Pastoral Reflections

A Collection of Sermons: Book 1

Kenneth P. Langer

Brass Bell Books

Brass Bell
Books & Games

Copyright © 2024 K. Langer

First Edition, September 2024

All rights reserved

No part of this book may be reproduced, or stored in a retrieval system, or transmitted in any form or by any means, electronic, mechanical, photocopying, recording, or otherwise, without express written permission of the publisher.

Published by Brass Bell Books and Games
www.brassbellbooks.com

Printed in the United States of America

I dwell in possibility
A fairer house than prose
More numerous of windows
Superior, for doors.

Of chambers as the cedars
Impregnable of eye
And for an everlasting roof
The gambrels of the sky

Of visitors, the fairest
For occupation – this
The spreading wide my narrow hands
To gather Paradise
EMILY DICKINSON

Contents

Title Page
Copyright
Epigraph
Introduction   1
The Sermons   6
Sermon 1   7
Sermon 2   13
Sermon 3   19
Sermon 4   25
Sermon 5   35
Sermon 6   45
Sermon 7   51
Sermon 8   58
Sermon 9   64
Sermon 10   70
Sermon 11   76
Sermon 12   82
Sermon 13   88
Sermon 14   93
Sermon 15   99

Sermon 16	103
Sermon 17	109
Sermon 18	115
Special Sermons	121
Special Sermon 1	122
Special Sermon 2	125
Acknowledgement	127
Other Books	129
Final Note	131

Introduction

A Little About The Author

(If you want to skip the part where I talk about myself, feel free to jump to the next section)

When I was much younger my mother used to take me grocery shopping with her. She would push her cart from aisle to aisle with me following behind. She took her food selection very seriously. Every item was carefully scrutinized so that she would choose the best foods for the best price. I am told I was mostly a quiet child so on some days my mother would traverse several aisles before she noticed I was no longer dutifully tagging along. When this happened she would have to turn around and search the between stacks of food to find me. When she did, I was often seen sitting on the floor scratching at a scrap piece of paper with a pencil. I was usually working on a poem or hastily writing down thoughts that had suddenly entered my mind. My mother would call my name in frustration and tell me to follow behind her. Instead of playing sports or chess or Kick The Can I wanted to create.

    I have always had two major interests in my life: the arts and religion. In fifth grade I began playing the trumpet in school and fell in love with music. I played in bands and, later, sang in choirs all through the rest of my school years until I decided to make music my major academic discipline. I received a Bachelor's and then a Master's degree in Music Education and then went on to get my doctorate in Music Theory and Composition.

Between teaching classes I composed a great deal of music for brass groups and choirs - ensembles with which I was most familiar. About halfway through my teaching career my composition activities slowed down and I took up writing. When I started to look back upon all the things I had written, both in music and literature, I began to notice a pattern. Most of the music I composed was focused on my growing pursuit of spiritual understanding. My switch to writing managed to help me express my ideas more concretely. I sometimes wondered if I had chosen the wrong life path.

Just before the onset of the Covid epidemic my life was altered dramatically to the point where I had to choose between giving up on everything or making a drastic change. I decided it was a chance to pursue something I never thought possible. I entered a Unitarian Universalist seminary to study theology.

I was introduced to Unitarian Universalism in the most unlikely of places: on a dusty road in the dark of night somewhere near the Okefenokee Swamp in southern Georgia. This was a place that had as many alligators as it did people and snow was rarely seen touching those brackish swamp waters. I was driving back to the small town where I found my first college teaching job when I heard on the radio the voice of someone who talked about religion. He was speaking many of the same thoughts I had but did not speak out loud in that very traditional and religiously conservative part of the country. At the end of the interview the speaker identified himself as a Unitarian Universalist minister. I had never heard of such a thing and the idea that there was an organized religious body who shared many of my ideas and feelings about religion was astounding to me. I started to attend UU churches wherever I went.

After three years of study during the midst of the pandemic when jobs were nearly impossible to find, I finished a Master's Degree in Divinity but then ran into another difficult challenge. In the UU tradition, any person can be ordained by any UU church but there is a process of Fellowship with the Unitarian Universalist Association that does or does not recommend a candidate for ordination. Without a full explanation I was denied Fellowship which meant I could not use the Association's system for applying to UU church positions. Fortunately for me, I found a church who accepted me despite the lack of Fellowship. That church was the First Church of Barre, Universalist in Barre, Vermont - also known as the Barre UU church. In my first year as their minister they ordained me as a Unitarian Universalist minister.

A Little About The Book

(This is the next section)

The sermons in this book are those I have given during my time at the First Church in Barre, Universalist (a Unitarian Universalist congregation). They are presented in the chronological order in which they were presented though some are related in topical series or are connected to events of the time. Through them and the music I often incorporate in services I bring to light many of the ideas and hopes I formulated over the years in brightly lit grocery aisles, stuffy campus buildings, mosquito filled swamps, and snow draped churches.

The focus of these sermons is not what one might expect from a minister in an old church. The Universalist Church in Barre dates back to the nineteenth century. Universalism was the sixth largest Christian denomination in the country by 1880 and the church in Barre was built during that time of rapid expansion. The Universalism of today, however, is much different than it was in those days. As Universalism grew it also ran into different spiritual traditions that were developing in America at the time. One of these was the group of people who would later be known as the Transcendentalists. Later, other influences of Universalist thought included the philosophy of Humanism, the development of scientific understanding, and issues of social justice as well as the knowledge of religious traditions throughout the world including Eastern, Native American, and Earth-Centered spiritualities led to a Contemporary Universalism that is non-creedal and open to people of all faiths and identities. My sermons are meant to reflect these more modern religious issues of our time.

Contemporary Universalism is, for the most part, non-Christian though many of its practices are derived from Christian traditions. Christmas, for example, is still a major traditional service of the year in many UU churches. These churches tend to use all religious traditions as well as modern sources of thought and philosophy to influence their services in churches that may be filled with people from many new and ancient religions traditions (such as the many forms of Christianity) or can include those with no tradition at all. The most difficult challenge of most UU ministers is to decide how to address the current conditions of our time to such a mixed collection of spiritual backgrounds.

The sermons in this collection reflect many of those current trends of the UU movement with a focus on my own personal views on religion and its meaning for life in this new century. My personal spiritual views can be called religious naturalism which is a spiritual view of nature and all life that does not include any supernatural influence.

Each of the sermons in this collection include a brief introduction about the sermon and its context. Some of them also include sources used in researching and writing them.

Many of the sermons in this collection belong to several different series of presentations. Many of the sermons are based upon a book I wrote while I was in seminary that helped me to focus my own spiritual understanding of the world. The book is entitled "The Emergence of God: The Intersection of Science,

Nature, and Spirituality". Many of the themes in that book became topics of separate sermons and further exploration.

Other series included days that were special because they celebrated a holiday or a special event, sermons that explained Unitarian Universalism, sermons based on themes proposed by the Soul Matters service, and sermons based on specific UU liturgical days or rituals.

The Sermons

Sermon 1

We Don't Talk About That: The Language of Reverence

Series: The Emergence of God

Delivered on September 24, 2023 at the Barre UU Church

Introduction

This was the first full sermon I gave at the Barre UU church. I was hired at a half-time level so I commuted back and forth between the Boston area and Barre which meant I had apartments in both places. I wanted to set out some premises of what I thought what my ministry should be about, namely, a proclamation of the sacredness of all things, a need to be more open about our faith and movement, a more expansive and inclusive view of the divine, an understanding of our past, and the use of a language of reverence.

The Sermon

I have been in Vermont now for only a few weeks and I have enjoyed getting to know each of you. When I meet people, the conversations have centered on details of our lives and our families, questions about past residences, and a brief review of educational backgrounds. Fortunately, most of you already know what I do. Recently, I have been reticent about answering the question about my new occupation with other people. Invariably, when I say I am a minister I can see their faces suddenly become very stiff. It's like watching a movie where the unwitting Greek stares into the face of the wicked Medusa. Medusa–as you may know–was a terrible mythical monster who had the face of a beautiful woman but whose hair was filled with snakes. The fate of any unfortunate human who saw her face was that they were immediately turned into stone That's the reaction I often get when I say the word 'minister.'

Why do people have such a visceral reaction to the word 'minister'? I think it's because people immediately make a range of assumptions about what it means to be a minister. They come with a set of preconceived notions such as: he is going to try and convert me, he is going to judge me, he is going to pontificate about the miserable condition of this sinful world. I have, however, found that I generally get a different reaction when I say that I am a Universalist minister. Instead of a hard face I get a quizzical look. "What's that?" they ask. I often respond with: "Well, we believe that all religions have some truth to them" to which I often get a response such as: "Oh, that's cool."

This is a problem we face as an alternative religion with a Christian heritage. We maintain some of the traditions and settings of our Christian past but without advancing the theology. The problem–in my humble opinion–is that we have dealt with that conundrum by completely rejecting our own narrative. We have eliminated our language of reverence.

Now, to understand the reasons why, I'd like to give you a brief historical review of how this came to be.

In the early 1800s when the evangelical movement known as the Second Great Awakening was raging across America, Unitarians railed against the literal biblical interpretations and the overt emotionalism that the church revivals brought out in people. They were afraid that this emotional fervor would override people's ability to think rationally and to remain independent. The Universalists resisted the frame of mind–espoused by the Calvinistic churches and others–who said that only some people were chosen at birth to be saved from damnation.

The Universalists insisted, instead, that all people were worthy of salvation. During this period, however, neither the Unitarians nor the Universalists abandoned their Christian framework. Instead, they cried out for a more expanded view of those teachings. That particular change was nudged on by the Transcendental movement which developed roughly around the same time near Concord, Massachusetts. The Transcendentalists encouraged people to find spirituality on their own. They were influenced from sacred sources other than the Bible and by other religions while they were also moved by a reverence for nature.

In the early twentieth century another movement became a strong influence on the Unitarians and the Universalists. This was the Humanist movement that came to the fore in the declaration of the first Humanist Manifesto of 1933. The humanists embraced reason and science and rejected so-called "God talk" and the supernatural aspects of religion. They helped to influence the Unitarian Fellowship movement in the mid 20th century.

The fellowship movement encouraged the development of new Unitarian congregations with a minimum of at least ten people in cities with a university. Those gatherings were lay-lead and their members tended to be humanists. That movement had a huge influence on the growth of Unitarian-Universalist churches in the South, the West, and the Midwest and greatly increased the total number of UUs across the country. As a result, the denomination overall became humanistic. Hymns were altered and re-written and new hymns were composed to reflect a more atheistic theology. UU services rejected many of the overtly Christian elements and Bibles were set aside to make room for influences from other sacred texts and other writers.

We humans tend to make changes throughout history by swinging the pendulum far in opposite directions. Instead of seeking balance, we throw everything out that reminds us of the past and then start all over again. Instead of finding common ground, we draw clear lines and take distant sides on issues. We focus on purely binary thinking and insist that we must either be Christian OR humanist, theists OR atheists, religious OR secular. As we find ourselves in the dawn of the 21st century we have begun to wonder if we have thrown out the baby with the holy water. When there are only two sides to an issue we create a steep cliff from which we can only teeter.

I am telling you all this because I once was on such a pinnacle. I found myself in the midst of a very difficult challenge in my life and felt horribly isolated and desolate. I was attracted to Unitarian Universalism in my twenties because of its atheistic humanism but, at that difficult moment in my life, I felt abandoned. I wanted to have that feeling of companionship and devotion that a loving god provided to others I knew but my dependence on reason did not allow for such beliefs. Part of the reason that I entered seminary was to help me find solutions to that dilemma.

The answers I did find I put together in my work "The Emergence of God" and many of the main ideas in that work will be the subject of future sermons. The work begins with explaining why a book on the intersection of science, nature, and spirituality includes the word God at all. I was unsure about using it because I knew that, for some, the word can invoke some anxiety–especially amongst other UUs.

I know that some amongst us have had unfortunate experiences with the church of their childhood. Clergy abuses have become news headlines in the past few decades. The image of an angry God has led to guilt, fear, and depression. The concept of a judgmental God has led to the oppression of minorities, the gender fluid, women, the marginalized, and, of course, those with differing theologies. So why did I choose to still use the word God in my book?

According to the Pew Research Center, most people go to church to feel closer to the divine - to God. The problem with that is that if the divine is narrowly defined by a small group of people, it becomes restrictive and exclusive. Religious fundamentalism in this country grew exponentially as a reaction against the counterculture movement of the 1960s and the Roe v. Wade decision of 1972. Since that time, the image of an anthropomorphic God capable of expressing hatred, or handing out favors, or justifying violence and war became the norm in American society. That narrow and–I would say–dangerous definition of God will remain the standard so long as people do not challenge it and THAT is the reason I chose to use the word myself.

For me, the divine is something more beautiful, more wonderful, more mysterious than that angry and judgmental God. It is greater and more grand than any single person or any one religion, or group of people, or country, or planet, or galaxy even. It is beyond race and gender and economic background and philosophy or theology or political persuasion. It is the source of beauty, the ground of being, and the wellspring of love. It is the endless fount of a continuous process of renewal and creativity. Sometimes I call this mysterious manifestation Spirit, Eternal Presence, Sacred One, or Cosmic Energy and sometimes I call it God because the term can imply a personal connection to the divine. That's what I needed when my world fell apart–something that could help me feel as if I was personally connected to the sacred.

All people need to feel connected, to feel whole, to be significant, to be loved for who they are. Some find it in their families, some seek it through their careers, and some find it in the vision of a loving and watchful God. I would never want to deny anyone of those feelings.

I wanted to use the language of reverence in my writing because I did not want to shy away from complex and enigmatic words. I wanted to redefine many of those spiritual terms so that they might be more inclusive, more accepting, and more spiritual. I wanted to push beyond simplistic and binary interpretations. I wanted people to know that they are all worthy and righteous enough to define these things for themselves. I wanted to encourage people to make their own sacred connection. I wanted to help people find what they needed to be well and whole.

That, I believe, is why we are here. It is why we gather here together. We lift each other up in our passions and our pains. We hold each other in our joys and our sorrows, We speak and we listen together. Whatever we may choose to call the divine, it is surely here. It is this moment. It is this place. It is all this.

Notes

1. "Why Americans Go To Church"
https://www.pewresearch.org/religion/2018/08/01/why-americans-go-to-religious-services/#:~:text=A%20new%20Pew%20Research%20Center,to%20feel%20closer%20to%20God.

Sermon 2

One Light Through Many Windows:

Contemporary Universalism

Series: Understanding Unitarian Universalism

Delivered on October 8, 2023 at the Barre UU Church

Introduction

In this sermon I wanted to explore the history of the Barre UU church. In particular I wanted to explore the historical influence of the Universalists who built it and kept it going. I believe we need to bring their Universalist principles into a more contemporary framework. My suggestion os to focus on three basic Universalist principles for our time. During this time the UUA was considering eliminating its seven basic principles and replacing them with six key principle words surrounded by the word "love".

I have always felt that few are able to remember all seven of those original principles but that reducing them to just seven words was not enough to remember or to act as a living principle. That is why I suggested just three from which all other principles could be a derived.

The Sermon

The theme for this month is Heritage. A heritage is literally something you inherit. As a church we have inherited a long history of Universalism. Despite our association with the Unitarian Universalist association our title remains First Church of Barre, Universalist. I was actually quite pleased when I found this out because only a year earlier I had been asked to guest preach at a church in Massachusetts and my topic was "Why I Choose To Call Myself a Universalist." In my last sermon here I related the fact that when people ask me what I do, I respond "I am a Universalist Minister." I have nothing against the Unitarian side of our UU history. It's just that I think that in these times we have come to more fully embrace the universalist side of our UU heritage. Also, the term "Unitarian Universalist" is a whopping ten syllables! The only other religious tradition that I know of that has ten syllables in its name is the Church of Jesus Christ of Latter Day Saints but they just call themselves Mormons.

It's a bit ironic that when the Unitarians and Universalists, two separate Christian denominations, chose to merge in 1961 to become the Unitarian Universalist Association, the Universalists quietly despaired. At that time, the Unitarians were the ones with more money, power, and influence than the Universalists. The Universalists were sure that the UUA merger would result in the eradication of their Universalist principles but it's the Unitarian insistence on one God that has diminished over time. As modern UUs, we do not require the belief in one god, or many gods, or any god. That is between you and your connection to the mysteries of this life. Being a UU is not dependent on your adherence to a particular belief. We define ourselves not by our words but through our actions. It is deeds not creeds that define us as people, as a church, as a country, and as citizens of this beautiful planet on which we live.

Those Universalists had good reason to grieve. In the midst of the Nineteenth century the Universalists were one of the largest Christian denominations in the United States but by the beginning of the twentieth century had become one of the smallest. In contrast, though, the Unitarians never reached the same level of membership though they were more influential. Their churches were more often located in or near large cities like Boston and were usually well funded. The Unitarians were considered the movers and the shakers of the liberal Christian world and often dominated the religious institutions of the time.

To some of those grieving Universalists, the merger of 1961 between Unitarians and Universalists was the only option left to sustain their movement but the act of merging with the Unitarians brought with it a high price. The combined UU Association would be dominated mostly by Unitarians for years to come. The Universalists were happy, however, that the word Unitarian came before Universalist in the joint name because they liked to consider the first word to be an adjective of the second. They were still Universalists but now they were a particular kind of Universalist: they were Unitarian Universalists.

This church here in Barre, Vermont was one of the first churches to develop in the heyday of Universalism in New England during the Nineteenth century. There was actually a separate Unitarian church in Barre at the time but it has not survived. The First Church in Barre, Universalist was formerly founded in 1796 but did not actually have a meeting house until one was built in South Barre in 1822. The building you are now sitting in (physically or virtually) was completed at this site in 1852. The growing popularity and influence of Universalism at the time led to the building of a Universalist seminary in 1870 at the location that is now the Barre City Auditorium. That seminary eventually moved out of Barre and later became known as Goddard College.

As interesting as this history might be you may be asking why it is important for us to better understand our heritage. I believe that, for one thing, we should be proud of our history but, secondly, and maybe more importantly, it is because I believe we should embrace our contemporary universalist theology. Martin Luther King once said "If we are to go forward today, we've got to go back and rediscover some mighty precious values that we've left behind ." In that spirit, let's take a moment and examine our Universalist heritage and what it may mean for us today.

The Universalists in this country began as a Christian denomination. Their philosophy was considered heretical by mainline Christians because it was based on the idea that every person was worthy of God's love. That truly meant everyone regardless of social position or church affiliation.

In an earlier manifestation, Universalists claimed that even though a person may be condemned to hell there would always be a way to find redemption. Universalists eventually rejected the idea of eternal damnation completely and decried that a loving God would never condemn any part of creation. Throughout the early part of the twentieth century, Universalist theologians began to accept the idea that true Universalism could not be centered on just one religion and the basic tenets of what I am calling contemporary Universalism were born.

Forrest Church was once the senior minister of the All Souls Church in Washington, D.C. He was ordained as a UU minister but liked to call himself a Universalist and often spoke about contemporary Universalism.

Rev. Church claimed that the foundations of contemporary Universalism must be grounded on the realities of the human condition. He highlighted three things that are true for all beings to which I am adding a fourth.

These four facts are true for every person and, indeed, every living being on this planet. They are valid regardless of background, economic condition, age, gender, political persuasion, cultural background, or number of Facebook friends. They have been true since the first cell split and will be true when the sun burns itself out. These essential truths are that 1) all living things must be born, 2) all living things must die, and 3) all living things are interrelated. It is because of these first three truths that the fourth truth arises which is that (4) all living beings will suffer. The only thing that is different for each being is how they will experience these realities. That means that every living being appears to be part of one grand pulsing existence.

These four fundamental actualities lead to a single basic theological revelation which is that there may be one source, one ground of being that may be called such things as the Mystery, the Great Spirit of Life, the Creator, the Divine, God or Goddess, the Buddha Nature, or our Joie de Vivre. This oneness is manifested in an ongoing and ever creative and diverse variety of manifestations. Rev. Church liked to use the analogy of the windows in a church. Though they may have many shapes and colors, the light behind them is the same. One light, many windows, he would say. I sometimes like to use the image of flowers for there are many beautiful blossoms that all arise from the same soil. One earth, many flowers.

Contemporary Universalism is based on these realities of life. It starts with the idea that we should live our lives according to the conditions of nature and our higher selves rather than through a story, parable, legend, or myth. To do that modern Universalists must have a different vision of the world. It is the vision of the brightly colored cathedral - Church's church.

I believe that vision is based upon at least three principles. These are 1) that ALL people are of equal worth and value, 2) that no one person or group or tradition can know the whole truth, and 3) that our survival and well-being are enhanced when we grow together in love. These three things can become the guiding principles by which a contemporary Universalist ethos may be guided and living them may be the best way (I believe) to promote those principles. Doing so gives our lives meaning, helps us to navigate the pains of life, and increases the possibility of finding and maintaining joy because it leads us into a connection to something beyond our individual selves. That is how I define religion. That is how I define contemporary Universalism. That is how I hope we will define ourselves as a congregation of Unitarian

Universalists.

If we look back at the heritage of our old and honored church and its traditions we can see that those same principles were essentially always there. Furthermore, those ideas are not solely derived from Christianity. Universal ideals have been expressed in works such as the Hindu Upanishads, the Buddhist Lotus Sutra, and the Sikh scripture called the Guru Granth Sahib.

So, we come back to the question: why is all this important? It is because I believe that the only way this world can move forward into peace and compassion for each other, for all beings, and for our planet, is to embrace contemporary Universalist principles. The only other option is to continue to disdain and destroy each other and our world. I believe these same principles will be the those upon which the church of the future will be shaped and I believe we can be the architects of that hopeful future.

Notes

1. "Early History of Barre Churches"

https://vermontgenealogy.com/washington/early-history-of-barre-vermont-churches.htm

2. *The Cathedral of the World: A Universalist Theology* by Forrest Church

Sermon 3

The Myth of Centrality: The Joy of Insignificance

Series: The Emergence of God

Delivered October 22, 2023 at the Barre UU Church

Introduction

My book The Emergence of God discusses several myths we have created and shared together that are not helpful in developing healthy and joyful living. This sermon discusses the first of these myths, one I call the myth of centrality, or the idea that we each individually and collectively (in our groups) consider ourselves the central focus of everything. I put forth the idea that this belief is both and concurrently true and not true.

The Sermon

In 1864, Jules Verne published the classic book entitled Journey to the Center of the Earth. In the book, a German scientist and his nephew delve into the heart of an extinct volcano in the hopes of finding the center of the earth. On their way, of course, they encounter a great number of dangers and challenges until they are finally ejected back to the surface. Why are we so intrigued and captivated by the center? One reason may be because of a myth that we have developed as a species–a myth I call the Myth of Centrality.

The Myth of Centrality is the idea that humanity is the center of the world. The fancy term for this is called "anthropic arrogance". This is a condition that has been maintained mostly, though not exclusively, through our Western culture. In fairness, the concept arises due to the way we experience the world. We all see everything primarily from the vantage points of our own bodies. From our viewpoint, everything revolves around us. Our senses alert us to things happening in front of us, behind us, or beside us. It takes a great deal of effort to see within or beyond ourselves. We can observe the stars, the sun, and the moon circling around us. We see the land extend outward in a flat plane in all directions from ourselves. The seas create artificial boundaries that surround the land.

Consider the following: the word China means "the middle country." If you translate the name of the Mediterranean Sea you literally get "middle earth". The Sioux have long considered the Black Hills of South Dakota to be the center of the world. In Tolkien's stories, Middle Earth is the land of the humans. There are many more examples of people who have identified a particular place as the center of the world.

Mountains have often been seen as a connection between earth and heaven in the center of the world. There are several such sacred mountains in the world. They are the Axis Mundi, the world pillar, or the cosmic center. They include Mt. Kailash - the residence of Shiva in the Himalayas, the sacred Kunlun mountains of China, the Shinto shrine of Mt. Fuji in Japan, Mt. Uluru in Australia - sacred to aboriginal tribes, Mt. Olympus in Greece - the home of the Greek gods, or the mystical Mt. Meru which is sacred to Hindus, Jains, Buddhists, and Taoists. Humanity has also constructed their own world pillars such as the Egyptian pyramids or the ziggurats in Mesopotamia. Some trees have been given the same honor including the mystical Celtic tree named Yggdrasil, the Banyan tree sacred to the Hindus, the famous Bo tree of India where the Buddha gained his enlightenment, or the Tree of Knowledge so central to the story in the book of Genesis. But, in the majority of world traditions created by humanity, the central concern is not focused on mountains or trees or buildings.

The primary concern of most religions is people - it is about us. We are at the heart and center of every religious story.

The dominant religious traditions of Western culture have perpetuated the idea of human centrality. From the Biblical book of Ezekiel we read: "Thus says the Lord God: This is Jerusalem; I have set her in the center of the nations, with countries all around her." Cities like Jerusalem, Rome, and Mecca were named the center of the world because the people who lived within them thought that where they lived was the most central location. From there, of course, it is easy to proclaim that your nation, your country, and your people must also occupy the world's focal hub.

When planets in our solar system were discovered we assumed that our little planet was the focal center of all of them, including the sun. In scientific terms this is known as the geocentric model of cosmology. This theory was prevalent well into the 16th century when Copernicus claimed that the sun was, in fact, the planetary center of the solar system rather than the earth. This is known as the heliotropic model. This idea was so heretical to the church that Copernicus waited to publish his findings until just before he died. When Galileo confirmed the findings of Copernicus, he was condemned by the Inquisition for heresy, was forced to recant, and was confined to his home for the rest of his life. When this dangerous idea was finally more broadly accepted, we then came to learn that ours was not the only solar system in the galaxy and it was Edwin Hubble who discovered that ours was not the only galaxy in the universe.

But, fear not! Our all-important need to be the center of attention did not wane as we embraced the galactocentric model of the universe and placed our own galaxy squarely in the center of everything. This assumption was made because it appeared that all the other galaxies were moving away from us. However, even this model has been proven to be incorrect. The easiest way to understand this is through the use of a very complex scientific instrument called... the balloon. [demonstrate] The surface of the balloon experiences an expansion in all directions. This is true regardless of where on the balloon you are looking. There is no center to the universe. The cosmos does not revolve exclusively around us.

This long-standing heritage of centrality has had some debilitating consequences in our culture. For one thing it can give us a sense of superiority. Such a sensibility brings with it judgments of good versus bad, better versus lesser, or us versus them. If we believe that our little corner of the world is the center of everything, then we can consider those other people outside of our sacred invisible circle we have created to be inferior. Those inside the circle are the good people and those outside are the bad people. In vs. out, good vs. evil, the right people vs. the wrong people, it's all the same thing. In the central circle, power structures emerge to maintain the boundary of the one true people. Even more focus is then concentrated on the center of the center–the leader.

This attention on one person can result in extreme acts of control and narcissism–something we have all seen recently in our own government. The problem becomes worse when there are several circles of people each of whom believes they are the center, the people of the truth, the righteous among the heathens. Wars have almost always been fought by those who claim they are right and must vanquish the wrong.

On a more personal level, we have been led to believe that we are each the center of our own universe. The world revolves around what we do, what we say, and how we look. We must each look our best, do our best, be the best in whatever we do.

Consequently, we have become a people of disillusionment and disappointment. We constantly try to live up to a model worthy of focus and scrutiny. We are the focus of our own attention but are never quite good enough to merit that attention. We separate ourselves and look for distractions. Recently, around 60% of all Americans have reported feeling lonely. We seek to fill the void caused by this separation by doing more, buying more, and saying more but it never ends the feelings of inadequacy. In fact, our consumerist economy is dependent on just this sense of inadequacy.

The real problem, though, is that when we are the center of the world, we leave no room for anything else. We separate the divine from ourselves, we devalue our relationships both to the sacred and to each other. We separate ourselves from the beauty and the contributions and the significance of the amazingly diverse world we live in. We even separate ourselves from the world itself. We have long believed that this planet is ours to do whatever we want. We have only recently begun to see the disastrous result of this vain presumption.

It has been said that the role of a minister is to comfort the afflicted and to afflict the comfortable so I am here to give you the bad news: neither you nor I are the center of the universe. We are not the center of the galaxy. We are not the center of the solar system. We are not the center of the world and we are not even the center of our own world. That's because, just as with the surface of the balloon, there is no center.

Now, I realize that this may sound like something disorienting but I am here to tell you it is not. We may not be the most important thing in the universe but there is a certain joy to insignificance. For one thing, we can begin to find out what is really significant in life. We can release the need to judge ourselves and others. We can gain a wider perspective on ourselves and our world. Without this judgment, without this need to constantly improve or impress or improvise, without this pressure to be more than we are, we can be free to be our authentic selves. We can embrace all the blemishes and flaws and imperfections that make us the unique and distinctive person that we are.

Perhaps more importantly than any of these things, the real joy of insignificance, is the chance to reach out to others and make the connections that are so important to the joy and happiness of being human. We can be there for others because we understand that each person is equally insignificant. We can both offer assistance and ask for help when needed because there is no longer a separation between those who deserve to be in and those who are not.

Now I am going to do something that ministers are not supposed to do. I am going to tell you that everything I just said was false. That's right, false. It was all wrong, bogus, baloney. It was all a lie; a polemic ruse. But I am obliged to tell you the real truth and this is it. You are the center of the world! That's right! You are the absolute center of the entire universe! But… so is the person next to you, and the person in front of you and behind you as is every person in Barre, or Berlin, or Bombay, or Beirut. Even now there are wars raging in the Middle East, and Ukraine, and Africa over land and religion and power because each side feels they have a certain right over others. The truth is that the center is everywhere, at every point, and in every place and person all the time.

That means you are significant, special, and exceptional–just like everyone else. And all these centers are interconnected like leaves on a tree or waves in the ocean. Each one is no less important than another. Each one is deserving of love and care and respect. Each one is beautiful in its own particular glory and splendor. But, I cannot express the idea any better than the Sufi poet Rumi who said: "Stop acting so small. You are the universe in ecstatic motion. Raise your words, not your voice. It is rain and not thunder that grows flowers. The very center of your heart is where life begins – the most beautiful place on earth. This is a subtle truth, whatever you love, you are."

Notes

1. *Journey to the Center of the Earth* by Jules Verne

Sermon 4

Getting Warm and Gooey: The Spiritual Practice of Generosity

Series: Soul Matters Themes

Delivered at the Barre UU Church on November 5, 2023

Introduction

The theme of the month for November was generosity. I decided to turn a card game I had invented as part of a book of original card games into a congregational activity. The game asks people to do a specific and simple act of kindness sometime during the month. The other point of the sermon was to demonstrate that kindness benefits both the receiver and the giver.

The Sermon

I was in line at the grocery store the other day. We've all been in line somewhere, some time. You know what it's like. Your mind drifts. You think about what you have to do next. You want to know why the line isn't moving. Don't these people know that I have other, more important things to do? My mind was drifting too until something cut through the noise. The woman at the check-out counter was getting into a panic. When I focused in I found out that she did not have enough cash for the groceries she selected and she did not have a credit card. She felt embarrassed and confused. She was short by about six dollars. The three people in front of me each handed the woman two dollars and she went on her way. I thanked those people as did the cashier and everyone else in line. Suddenly, another tedious wait in another nondescript line at a fluorescent box store became a beautiful moment of sharing and kindness and generosity. That is the focus of this sermon today: generosity.

Since this IS a UU sermon, we will most properly begin with a definition of the generosity. The website Wiktionary defines generosity as "The trait of being willing to donate money, resources, or time." The University of Notre Dame has something they call The Science of Generosity Project where they actually study the topic in detail. They define generosity as "giving good things to others freely and abundantly." It would be interesting to know how much free and abundant grant money it took to come up with that definition.

Perhaps the most surprising definition to me was from the Merriam Webster Dictionary which states that a generous person is someone who is "liberal in giving." Oh my! Someone used the word 'liberal.' The same source says that the word 'liberal' implies "openhandedness in the giver and largeness in the thing or amount given." So it turns out that 'liberal' is not a dirty word but then neither is 'conservative' because, as it turns out, one's political view does not determine who is more likely to be generous. According to the National Academy of Science, politically left-leaning and right-leaning people may donate to different types of organizations but both can be very generous in giving.

Unfortunately, the word 'generous' like the word 'liberal' has gotten a bad rap in our culture. Some of this is attributed to poor Darwin who is reported to have coined the idea that evolution is a process of survival of the fittest. The truth is, however, that the phrase was created by the English philosopher and psychologist Herbert Spencer. Spencer's comment was taken to mean that only the strongest and the toughest can survive. This has been the directive behind the image of the rugged American individualist.

Generosity became a sign of weakness; a weak link in the progress of evolution. But, organizations such as the Greater Good Science Center as well as other research psychology centers have demonstrated that survival of the species depends more on the overall fitness of the community rather than the individual. They found that a diverse community is able to depend on the varied and unique abilities of its people to overcome the various challenges involved in living a good life now and into the future. In short, we are better able to survive when we work together. This is all well and good but most people do not engage in generous acts of giving with the overall health of the community in mind. Most people tend to give for more personal reasons or, should I say, for more selfish reasons. In actuality, generosity is often a selfish act.

Now there's another word with a bad rap. The word 'selfish' often connotes a sense of uncaring arrogance. To call someone selfish is an insult. It is an unfortunate attitude leftover from our Puritan heritage where a focus on personal well being was always suspect. It is my opinion that doing something for yourself is only immoral, or sinful (if you will) if in doing that act you purposely or inadvertently cause harm to others. There's nothing wrong with enjoying a good meal with others so long as you do not eat everything in sight while others are left hungry.

It is possible for giving to be beneficial for both the giver and the receiver at the same time. It is possible to give while also receiving because doing good can also feel good. Being good to yourself because you are being good to others is not selfish. As a Psychology Today article put it: "Generosity is a good thing for our mental health and well-being because when we give to someone we care about, we make it more likely for them to give to us, making us more likely to give to them, and so on. As a result, regions of our brain associated with pleasure, social connection, and trust light up, making us feel all warm and gooey inside." And who doesn't want to feel all warm and gooey?

It turns out that science has determined that being generous benefits both the recipient and the donor. Specifically, it has been demonstrated that being generous can reduce stress because your body actually rewards you for doing good. When generous, chemicals such as endorphins, dopamine, and oxytocin are released into the bloodstream. According to the research, this may be because the body learned to reward behavior that was socially advantageous. Believe it or not, a group of compassionate and cooperative people tend to survive better than does a murderous angry mob. Who knew?

As you might imagine, being generous tends to improve relationships both individually and collectively. I think it can be said that the strength of a friendship can be measured by how generous those companions are to each other in time, thought, and resources. If that same kind of magnanimity can be extended outward into wider circles of relationship, an entire community could benefit. It helps that generosity has also been found to be contagious. After experiencing an act of goodwill, most people tend to want to repay the gift in kind. According to a paper published by the National Library of Medicine, "generous decisions engage the temporo-parietal lobe." In other words, there is a neural link between kindness and happiness.

Now, connected neural pathways are certainly a good and fine thing to have but I am personally more interested in even greater connected pathways afforded through generosity. Those are pathways to the divine–to the sense of something greater than our individual selves. Those of us who seek that kind of mystical connection often do so through spiritual practices. Generosity can be one such spiritual practice.

If you think about it, generosity is actually part of every spiritual practice. Whether you meditate, sing sacred songs, pray, spin around like a whirling dervish, or hug trees in the forest, the desire to engage in a spiritual practice begins with a generous act to yourself. You are giving yourself the gift of transcending your individuality and finding deeper meaning to your life. As you grow and mature spiritually, you learn the significance of being in a meaningful relationship with others. Your circle of caring expands outwards from yourself towards greater and greater domains of beings. In the process, you may also learn more and more about yourself. You may encounter your own fears about being connected to others. You may engage with your own confused feelings about reciprocity. You may come to realize that true giving does not expect something in return and that the spiritual practice of generosity is its own reward. You may further come to understand how being generous is actually a gift you give to yourself.

So now you have listened to me wax poetically about generosity and to say all the things you probably expected me to say but now it's time to put the rubber to the road, to put your shoulder to the wheel, to get the ball rolling, as it were, because I want to dare you to take my Kindness Challenge. In my book of original card games–52+ Card Games–I came up with something called the Kindness Game. In the version I will present to you here, I am challenging you to engage in an act of kindness dictated by a playing card.

I have a deck of cards with the name of our church printed on them. I also have a list of simple acts of generosity connected to the playing cards. All of this is also available on the church website for those who want to join us or if you forget your objective. Please go to our Activities page to find this Acts of Kindness Game. I challenge you to take and keep a random card. When you look at the card, find the suit and number on the sheet and find the act connected to it. My challenge to you is that you do that random act of kindness and that you do it anonymously. Then, I challenge you to take a picture of the card in a setting that displays something related to your act of kindness. Finally, I ask that you send that picture to me so that I can post it online and have a collection of pictures related to the challenge. You are also welcome to invite others to join our challenge so that we can build a great photo gallery of our project.

For example, let's say you pulled the Ace of Spades. You would look at the Kindness game sheet and see that the related activity is to compliment someone you do not know. The next day you walk down the street and say to a stranger that they look good and the stranger thanks you. If you get their permission, you could then take a photo of you and the stranger, or just them. or just you, and the place where it happened, and then send that photo to the church so that we can post it.

Let us now go forth and be generous!

Notes

1. "University of Notre Dame Science of Generosity Project" https://generosityresearch.nd.edu/

2. The Greater Good Science Center

https://greatergood.berkeley.edu/

3. The Real Challenge of Generosity by Wayne Baker. Psychology Today January 13, 2020.

https://www.psychologytoday.com/us/blog/master-your-success/202001/the-real-challenge-generosity

4. A Neural Link Between Generosity and Happiness. National Library of Medicine, July 11, 2017

https://www.ncbi.nlm.nih.gov/pmc/articles/PMC5508200/

The Kindness Game:

♠ Spades

- [A♠] Compliment someone you don't know.
- [2♠] Write a friendly note to someone.
- [3♠] Give someone a small gift.
- [4♠] Give someone a note with a compliment on it.
- [5♠] Find a busy street and fill it with bubbles.
- [6♠] Ask for someone's autograph.

- [7♠] Donate some money to a worthy cause you have not supported before.

- [8♠] Put a friendly note on someone's car.

- [9♠] Put a friendly note in someone's mailbox.

- [10♠] Deliver flowers to a nursing home or hospital.

- [J♠] Listen to someone without interrupting or offering solutions.

- [Q♠] Donate some of your old stuff.

- [K♠] Donate food.

♡ Hearts

- [A♡] Take a selfie with someone you don't know.

- [2♡] When you pay for something (like coffee or lunch) pay for the next person's as well.

- [3♡] Post a positive sign in an unusual place.

- [4♡] Give a random person a $5 gift card.

- [5♡] Post a whole pack of sticky notes with positive messages in random places.

- [6♡] Clean trash in a public place.

- [7♡] Compliment a parent for having a well-behaved child.

- [8♡] Bring extra food to a dog or cat shelter or volunteer in some other way.

- [9♡] Do something special for a waitstaff or server person (and give a good tip).

- [10♡] Write a positive or supportive comment for someone on a website or blog.

- [J♡] Donate something you no longer need.

- [Q♡] Compliment a stranger on his/her appearance.
- [K♡] Smile at five people for no reason.

♣ Clubs

- [A♣] Support a locally produced art show or studio by a local artist by purchasing a work or complementing the artist.
- [2♣] Support a locally produced theater performance by attending or volunteering. Give compliments to the performers.
- [3♣] Support a locally produced musical production such as a school concert. Offer compliments to the director and the performers.
- [4♣] Find any kind of local event such as a farmer's market or festival and offer to volunteer, participate, or attend.
- [5♣] Leave some quarters in random locations like the sidewalk, near parking meters, the laundromat, or snack machines.
- [6♣] Leave shiny new pennies (heads-up) in a place near where kids travel or visit.
- [7♣] Drop a note in a mailbox to tell someone their home looks nice.
- [8♣] Lend your talents to someone for free.
- [9♣] Promote someone else's work to people.
- [10♣] Contact someone you have not seen in a long time.
- [J♣] Offer to freely help someone do something they need done.
- [Q♣] Place random kind notes in different books at

the library.

- [K♣] Leave a small gift on someone's doorstep.

◇ Diamonds

- [A◇] Write positive messages in chalk on the sidewalk or on a poster.

- [2◇] Hand out lottery tickets (or some other kind of inexpensive ticket) to strangers.

- [3◇] Hold a sign that says "hello" then wave at people passing by in their cars.

- [4◇] Offer a small gift like cookies or a gift card to a sanitation worker, custodian, or other person that is often ignored.

- [5◇] Volunteer at a soup kitchen or other local service group.

- [6◇] Put a kind into a copy of a book you have enjoyed and set the book in a place where someone might find it like on a train or bus.

- [7◇] Do something you think would honor the memory of someone you or a loved one has lost.

- [8◇] Buy some extra food at the grocery store to donate to a food shelter.

- [9◇] Send a thank-you note to someone who has done something for you or someone else.

- [10◇] Make something then give it to someone.

- [J◇] Do your best to spend an entire day without complaining.

- [Q◇] Volunteer to do someone else's chore.

- [K◇] Exercise patience for an entire day regardless of what happens.

KENNETH LANGER

∞∞∞

Sermon 5

Yuletide Readings and Carols

Series: UU Liturgy

Given at the Barre UU Church on December 17, 2023

Introduction

It has become a tradition in many Christian churches to do an annual service during the Winter Holidays known as Christmas Lessons and Carols. I wanted to begin a similar tradition in our church using music and stories to highlight the return of the light we experience at the Winter Solstice.

The Sermon

The tradition of caroling is an ancient one. Throughout Europe and America, small groups of singers would travel from home to home and sing carols well into the nineteenth century. Their familiarity and popularity eventually brought them into the church worship service. In 1878, St. Paul's Cathedral in London hosted a "Choral Evensong" that included carols for the season. Two years later a Christmas service with nine lessons and carols about the story of Jesus began as a way to discourage people from hitting the pubs during the holiday season. This special service gained great fame when it began to be performed at King's College in Cambridge, England starting in 1918.

Today we will enact our own service of readings and carols in four parts to honor the season of Yule and the story of the rebirth of the sun that happens every year at the Winter Solstice. Through tales, poetry, and music from around the world, we will tell the story of the return of the light and warmth of the sun - an event that has brought joy to people of many ages and many cultures throughout the ages and as it still does today.

Though we usually rise at the singing of our hymns, I will invite you to remain seated and comfortable until we sing the last one of this series.

Part I: The Sun Has Died

The Summer Solstice is in June in the Northern hemisphere and from its inception, the light of the sun begins to fade to us. The change is slow and gradual and we often do not really take notice until late October. Part of the reason we have Halloween is because it is a time when people recognize that the dark and cold part of the year is about to begin. To those who may not have not been sure that the sun would ever actually return, such a time was very frightening. Short days, long and dark nights, winds that howl in anguish and bite our skin with a bitter chill, and the appearance of rigid snow and ice that falls from the sky like desperate tears makes it seem like the sun has died and even the earth and sky weep upon its demise.

Susan Cooper's Poem, The Shortest Day, has become a traditional reading in many UU churches at this time of year. It speaks of how people have long fought against the fear and anxiety of the darkness before the Winter Solstice through singing, decorations, and a rekindling of hope.

[Read: Susan Cooper's poem "The Shortest Day"]

So now the shortest day approaches, the evenings grow longer, and the sun withers away. It feels as if this season is the long dark evening of the year.

Let us sing our first carol - hymn no. 46 "Now The Day Is Over"

The Inuit Tribes have long lived in many of the coldest parts of

North America. They often share a story at this time of year to tell how Raven has stolen the light.

Tupilak was a magician that lived in a far cold and snowy mountain. One day he decided to steal the sun so he climbed his snowy mountain and reached up into the sky. With his magic he was able to pull down the sun and put it in a bag. Then he hid the bag in a secret place behind the sky.

Below the mountain the days became colder and colder and food became more and more scarce. People were freezing and starving so they went to the trickster Raven for help. Raven agreed to help the people. He gathered as many rocks as he could carry and flew up toward the sky with all his might. As he flew across the ocean, he dropped one rock at a time in the water. Each rock formed into an island where he could rest for a short while before continuing on his flight.

After a long journey he found a hole in the sky and flew into it. There he found the hidden bag with the sun inside. As he was gathering the bag he noticed Tupilak's beautiful daughter drinking water beside a flowing stream. Raven turned himself into a tiny feather and dropped himself into the water. Tupilak's daughter drank the water with the feather in it.

Months later Tupilak's daughter gave birth to a young son who was actually Raven in disguise. The child cried and demanded to play with the bag that contained the sun and so his mother gave it to him. Raven opened the bag and released the sun into the skWhen Tupilak found out the sun was gone he was mad and went to get it back. Now every year Tupilak steals the sun and Raven becomes a new child and takes it back. It is said that every time a baby cries at birth, it is a reminder of Raven's gift of the sun.

The birth of Raven and the gift of the light of the sun is celebrated through the miracle of every birth. The birth of a child and the rebirth of the sun are both chances to have new hope for the future.

Let us sing our second carol - hymn no. 234 "In The Gentle of the

Moon"

Part II: People Look East

The light of the sun has been stolen and now the darkness and the cold descends upon us but it is in the hope and realization of the sun's return that we find joy in this difficult time of the year.

Anthony Perrino's Poem "A Gentle Kind Of Gladness" speaks to that sense of quiet anticipation of this time of year. People look to the dark sky and forget their hatreds and pains. They look for a sign of the impending light. They look for a glimmer of hope that arises in the East.

[Read Anthony Perrino's poem "A Gentle Kind Of Gladness"]

It is in the East that the new sun will be born. It is there that a bright star will rise and lighten the barren lands. That light upon the snow covered hills is hope and that light within our hearts is love.

To encourage and welcome its return we fill places with evergreens and lights. At first those lights were fires but now they are electric and can twinkle or be filled with bright colors.

Please join me in singing our third carol - hymn no. 226 "People Look East"

Our next story is about a woman who searches for the Child of Light and it comes from Italy.

Befana is an old woman who lives alone in a cabin in the woods. Everyday she sweeps out her cabin with a long thin broom made from a crooked tree branch and stalks of hay. One day a procession of people passed by her cabin as she was sweeping. A small boy from the parade noticed Befana sweeping away. He broke off from the others and ran toward her.

"We are looking for the Child of Light," he said. "Have you seen it?" Befana did not look up but just kept sweeping slow and steady. "We are looking for the Child of Light but cannot find it anywhere. Can you help us?" the boy implored. "Go away, go away!" Befana crackled.

"Can't you see I'm busy?" But, the boy insisted: "It is the child that will light up the whole world, that is why we must find it." Befana said nothing.

Frustrated, the young boy rejoined the procession as it made its way out of town. Befana kept sweeping but thought about what the young boy had said. She was curious about this Child of Light. Would it bring light to the whole world, she wondered. What joy and happiness such a child would bring to everyone. She remembered how excited the young boy was as he told her about this child and it got her thinking. Suddenly she lit up with such great delight at the thought of finding this Child of Light.

The whole cabin came alive as Befana started baking up as many wonderful cookies and pies and cakes as she could. She started singing and dancing all throughout the small house. When she was done she packed away as many of the baked goods as she could carry then she waited until dark so that no one would see her. She grabbed her stick broom and flew up into the night sky all the while laughing and hooting. She flew and flew but had no idea how to find this Child of Light so she flew to the house of every child she could find and left some baked goods for them to find in the morning just in case one of those children happened to be the Child of Light.

We all look for the Child of Light on the solstice. The new sun is like a newborn child that is full of wonder and dreams. It rises in the East and we seek it out in the dark just as the three wise men sought out the birth of their prophet. They left their lands to seek out the Child of Light.

In our next hymn, even the shepherds are advised by the angels to leave their flocks for a time so that they can follow the rising star to the east.

Please join me in singing our fourth carol - hymn no. 255 "There's A Star In The East"

Part III - The Sun Is Reborn

On the third day after the solstice the sun appears to stop

descending and begins again to rise. It is as if it has been reborn. From that day forward to the summer solstice each day will hold just a little more light and though the warmth of Spring will take time to reach us, the lengthening days give us the promise that it will arrive.

Margaret Atwood, in her poem entitled Shapechangers In Winter writes of the this time of year when she says,

[Read Margaret Atwood's poem Shapechangers In Winter.]

The day the sun is reborn is, indeed, a time to be joyous and grateful. In our next hymn we sing how the hope of earth is awakened once again at the rising of the new sun.

Please join me in singing our fifth carol - hymn no. 236 "O Thou Joyful Day".

In this story from Tanzania, the creatures of the land realize they must work together to bring back the light on the day they called the "Pull-Together Morning".

Deep in the jungle everybody noticed that it had become dark. The sky went without sunshine. Everyone needed light to see where they were going. They kept bumping into trees and falling into holes. They would bump into each other and then great fights would break out. Things were getting confusing. Tempers flared and some were scared. Something had to be done so Lion called a meeting. Everyone came to the meeting including Elephant and Mouse, Giraffe and Zebra, Antelope, Monkey, Cobra, Crocodile and even Spider and Fly. As they talked and argued, Monkey noticed a hole in the sky. "Look," said Monkey. "There's a tiny hole in the sky and there's light in that hole." Everyone looked up to where Monkey was pointing.

"We must get to that hole," said Elephant. "And see if we can bring down that light." "I can get through that hole," said Fly. "But it's too far for me to fly with my tiny wings."

Lion looked toward the crowd then spoke. "Crocodile can swim out to the ocean with Giraffe on her back. Cobra can crawl up Giraffe's

back and carry Mouse as high up as they can go. Cobra will stretch out as far as he can go so that Spider can go very high and shoot her web toward the hole. Fly can crawl up that web as far as it goes and then fly the rest of the way until she reaches the hole in the sky.

"But," protested Fly. "Spider will eat me before I even get up there." Before Lion could even respond, Spider cried out "And Cobra will eat me." "Not before Giraffe tramples all over me," said Mouse. "Well," said Giraffe as he lowered his head from the sky. "None of you will have anything to worry about because Crocodile will consume me before we can even get started."

"Then," roared Lion. "We must learn to work together. We will each have to give up what we need individually and focus on what we need to bring back the light together or we shall all be doomed to walk in the dark forever."

Everyone nodded and agreed to work together and, eventually, Fly made it through the tiny hole. Behind that hole lived the King of Light. Fly was able to discover that the King had placed their light in a box so everyone worked together to help Fly steal the box and bring it back to the world below. There they opened the box. But instead of light - out popped Rooster.

"Where's the light?" They all called but Rooster just stood tall and then bellowed out, "Harambee" which in Swahili means "Let's all pull together." Suddenly the sun rose over the horizon and filled the world with light.

The birth of the sun at the solstice reminds us of the miracle and wonder of every birth. Sophia Lyon Fahs reminds us of this in her poem, Each Night A Child Is Born.

[Read Sophia Lyon Fahs' poem Each Night A Child Is Born.]

With the birth of every child from every land we get a glimpse of the pure light of all life. Each new life gives us a chance to welcome love and to extend hope for an age of peace.

Please join me in singing our sixth carol - hymn no. 238

"Within the Shining of A Star".

<u>Part IV: The Light of Peace and Love</u>

When the solstice has passed and the light is reborn, we look forward to a new year of growth and renewal. In a story entitled The Rebirth of the Sun, Starhawk writes:

"Early in the morning, the old ones woke the children. Together they climbed a high hill and faced to the east, the direction of sunrise. They sang songs to the sun and ran around trying to keep warm. They waited and waited to see what dawn would bring.

The sky began to turn from black to indigo to blue. Slowly the sky grew light. A golden glow crept over the horizon. Night opened her great arms, and in a burst of brightness, the sun appeared, new and strong and shining.

For in the long night the sun had rested well and grown young from the songs and the thanks of the children, young as a brand-new baby, born out of Night once more. Everybody cheered, and the children jumped up and down.

"The sun has returned! The sun is reborn!" the people cried. And they danced and sang to celebrate the birth of a new day, and then went home for breakfast."

In our next hymn, the angels come from heaven to promise us a time of peace and goodwill in the midst of the dark. If only we would pause to hear their beautiful music and find peace in our own hearts.

Please join me in singing our seventh carol - hymn no. 244 "It Came Upon The Midnight Clear"

Our next story is from the !Kung people of the Kalahari desert region of southern Africa. During the Winter months they gather around a common location and cease their travels. There they share stories to pass the time until Spring returns. This is one of those stories. It is the story of Grandfather Mantis.

For as long as people could remember the Sun Man brought light and warmth to the land but one day the Sun Man began to get old and tired. Every morning he rose just a little bit later and every night he went to bed just a little bit earlier. As the days got darker people began to get cold and listless. They turned from happy to sad. They went to visit the wise old one known as Grandfather Mantis for help. Grandfather Mantis was also old and tired and just wanted to be left alone but the people begged him so he came up with an idea.

He called together all his children and grandchildren. He told them to find Sun Man sleeping in bed and then, with all their might, they should throw him into the sky. This the children did and with all the strength they could gather together they threw Sun Man out of his bed and into the sky. Sun Man flailed about and all his thrashing caused light to spread through the land. Sun Man came to life and gave light to the people again. The people rejoiced. They put on their finest clothes because now they could see each other and they no longer needed heavy coats. So they came together in their colorful outfits and celebrated and feasted.

We, too, celebrate this time of year regardless of culture, creed, or background because the return of the light of the sun is a wonderful time for all beings in this world.

As a writer and former president of the Starr King School for the Ministry, Rebecca Ann Parker best captures the Unitarian Universalist sense of joy we find in the Winter Solstice when she writes:

[Read Rebecca Ann Parker's poem: Winter Solstice]

Please rise in body or spirit and join me in singing our eighth and final carol - hymn no. 245 "Joy To The World"

Notes

1. All hymns are from the UU hymnbook: "Singing The Living Tradition".

2. All the stories were adapted from the book: *The Return of the Light: Twelve Tales from Around the World* by Carolyn McVickar Edwards

KENNETH LANGER

Sermon 6

Love Will Always Liberate: The Love Theology of Martin Luther King, Jr.

Series: Special Days

Delivered at the Barre UU Church on January 14, 2024

Introduction

This sermon was meant to combine a message of love for Valentine's Day and the specific spiritual message of love that was at the heart of Martin Luther King's ministry. It begins by mentioning the fact that Martin and Coretta considered joining a local Unitarian church (not a UU church since this was before 1961). I then ask people to reflect upon the reasons why the Kings decided not to join the church.

The Sermon

Did you know that Dr. Martin Luther King Jr. once considered the possibility of becoming a Unitarian? It's true. He had, after all, done his doctoral studies in theology at Boston University in the city that houses the national headquarters of the Unitarian Universalist Movement. He had studied the works of the transcendentalist Henry David Thoreau, and religious naturalist and Unitarian theologian Henry Nelson Weiman, among other contemporary philosophers.

Imagine it: one of the greatest American leaders of our nation

- someone committed to social change through non-violence; a brilliant orator and organizer; a man who dedicated his life to peace and equality; a winner of the Nobel Peace Prize, the Presidential Medal of Freedom, and the Congressional Gold Medal, among other awards - and he might have become a Unitarian Universalist! But, it was not to be.

Before Coretta Scott King met her future husband in Boston she had attended Unitarian churches for many years. Even after they were married, Coretta and Martin attended several Unitarian churches. Despite that fact, the Kings did not become members of any UU church because, as Coretta said, "We gave a lot of thought to becoming Unitarian at one time, but Martin and I realized we could never build a mass movement of black people if we were Unitarian."

Think about that for a moment. Dr. King did not join our ranks because he was concerned that it would negatively impact his ability to relate to the plight of Black Americans. Negatively impact! What does that say about us? We, as Unitarian Universalists, have long been proud of our stance on social equality and racial justice. We have spoken about these things long before our Association came together in 1961 but our words have not always matched our actions. The UU historian and author Mark Morrison Reed writes, "Prior to the 1960s most members of both denominations (that is, the Unitarians and Universalists) had little contact with African Americans as equals, knew nothing substantive about their culture, and the awareness that they should be concerned with racial injustice and inequality was only slowly dawning." In short, our ideals were not revealed through our actions.

The UUA only formed the Commission on Religion and Race in 1963 - eight years after the bus boycotts in Birmingham, Alabama and the same year as the famous March on Washington D.C. led by Dr. King in which he delivered his famous "I have A Dream" speech. In 1969, the UUA was nearly split in two when delegates at the General Assembly meeting in Boston walked out in protest of what they called "racist votes". Our words then certainly did not match our actions.

I think the reasons that Dr. King did not become a UU are important to us and something we should consider as we honor his legacy because those reasons are as much about us as they are about him. Why DID King turn away from the liberal religious tradition and, instead, embrace his Southern Baptist roots? In an essay, King once wrote, " I came to feel that liberalism had been all too sentimental concerning human nature and that it leaned toward a false idealism... Liberalism failed to see that reason by itself is little more than an instrument to justify man's defensive ways of thinking." In other words, we UUs tend to be more in our heads than in our hearts. We are more fancy words than compassionate action.

King, of course, had been brought up in the customs and practices of African-American theology and the Black Protestant church. In both of these traditions, God is relational and not just conceptual. For King, God was the force of love itself and Jesus was the model of how to overcome suffering through love. What he called the three great evils of society: poverty, racism, and war, were, to him, failures of the human heart that could only be overcome through the power of love. Through this divine power,

King believed all people were connected and interdependent. Because of this very intertwined relationship, King felt deeply and strongly that hatred and violence could never be the answer to change because those things only caused more pain and deeper rifts in the fabric of all life. Hatred brings only more hatred and violence brings only more violence and both do no more than create downward spirals of suffering. Only love, he believed, could end this cycle of anger and hatred. In King's own words, "Darkness cannot drive out darkness; only light can do that. Hate cannot drive out hate; only love can do that."

What this meant for Martin Luther King was that the only

way to fight against the incredible injustices being done to African Americans was to wear down the hatred of others with love. He taught the people who followed him to not fight back in anger but to resist without hatred. No matter what was done to them they were to not return anger for anger nor violence for violence. He depended on the long term solution of non-violence over the short term fix of vengeance.

He focused on tactics of peace he learned not in the academic halls of Boston but from the quiet voice of a Hindu man who ousted the British government from his country - Mahatma Gandhi. King once said that "Christ gave us the goals and Mahatma Gandhi gave us the tactics." Quoting from the Bible, King would often say that people who do this work of non-violent resistance and justice seeking must combine the wisdom of the serpent but be as harmless as the dove. King believed that hatred was its own burden that weighed down upon those who carried it. Those filled with hate will always be consumed and defeated by it. The burden of hatred cannot be used to defeat more hatred.

What he was asking of his people was to fight hatred with love, to resist anger with compassion, and to repel violence with a steadfast calm. It seems almost superhuman to imagine such strength but that was what he said was required to build lasting peace and justice. He once wrote, "Send your hooded perpetrators of violence into our community at the midnight hour and beat us and leave us half dead, and we shall still love you. But be assured that we will wear you down by our capacity to suffer. One day we shall win freedom, but not only for ourselves."

Freedom! But not only for ourselves! THAT is the point, here! What Dr. Martin Luther King preached about was something that touches upon the lives of ALL people regardless of color or religion or economic condition. He called aloud for the freedom and justice of every human being everywhere because he believed that we are all intimately connected to each other. Hatred toward one is hatred toward all. Anger toward one is anger toward all.

Suffering brought upon one causes suffering to all. And each is a wound to the tender body of all of humanity. The freedom of some can never be gained without the freedom of all.

We all seek peace, justice, understanding, and compassion. We all seek to be loved but we let our fears overcome our need for love. Fear breeds confusion and anger and a desire to lash out against those we perceive to be our enemies but the only enemy is the fear that fuels the rage and the only way to overcome fear is through love.

King firmly believed that the divine was at the heart of every being and every person, black or white, Southerner or Northerner, liberal or conservative. Our failing as a people, as he saw it, was that we do not see that innate divinity and, instead, focus on our own self-centered needs and fears. He used the Greek term agape to define this kind of inner love that connects us all together as part of the same sacred unity.

If you believe, as Martin Luther King did, that all people - regardless of color, or background, or culture, or means - are equally part of the same being of love then you must find a way to love in the same manner. Such love, said King, requires that we forgive those who hurt us. Such love requires that we remember that all people are capable of both good and evil actions - including ourselves. Such love requires us not to return evil with evil but to do what we can to always offer people a chance for redemption. Such love resists the desire to seek vengeance on others regardless of what they may have done. Such love seeks only more love even in the presence of hatred. Anything else only builds barriers to peace.

This type of powerful and redemptive love is only possible when we view the world as one being. It is only possible when we engage both our heads AND our hearts. It is only possible when we can be both wise serpent as well as gentle dove. It is only possible when we speak about peace and then follow up our words with our actions. It is only possible when we act through, and with, and in, love.

Notes

1. "To Pray Without Apology: What would have happened if Martin Luther King Jr. had cast his lot with the Unitarian Universalists? A Reflection on Race and Theology." by Rosemary Bray McNatt

2. "The UUA Meets Black Power." By Warren A Ross

3. *King: A Life* by Jonathan Eig (a biography)

4. *Strength To Love* by Martin Luther King Jr. (A collection of sermons)

5. *The Selma Awakening: How The Civil Rights Movement Tested and Changed Unitarian Universalism* by Mark Morrison Reed

Sermon 7

The Ghost in the Pusheen: Contemporary Universalism

Series: Understanding Unitarian Universalism

Delivered at the Barre UU Church on January 28, 2024

Introduction

This sermon follows the discussion of contemporary Universalism given in sermon two. Since the merger of 1961, Unitarian Universalism has struggled to define itself. The heritage of both Unitarians and Universalists is rooted in liberal Christianity but has emerged as a multi-spiritual tradition. I think that we can still identify ourselves through a more modern understanding of the two terms used to name the movement.

The sermon begins with a discussion on the wisdom and spirituality of cats – at least as we may perceive their actions. Later I suggest that the word Unitarian refer not to a particular tradition but to the word "unity' embedded within it. This would require a rejection of dualities such as the concept of mind-body duality or the idea that the mind and body are separate. The fallacy of this thinking is illustrated when one asks what the mind if not just a ghost in the machine of the body.

To bring the discussion back to the spiritual cat I turned the phrase into a ghost in the Pusheen – a stuffed cat popular with kids at the time.

The Sermon

As Unitarian Universalists we believe that spirituality can be found in many ways and in many places. We seek wisdom and inspiration from a variety of sources, including sacred texts, the wisdom of artists, the stories of great people, the beauty of nature, and cats - yes cats! It turns out that we can learn a lot about spirituality from cats. Let me share with you the wisdom of the sacred feline with the following tips to enlightenment and purrrfection.

1) Take a lot of naps. Sleeping often in a warm sunny spot is very important to our mental, physical, and spiritual health.

2) Bathe often. Cleanliness is, indeed, next to Godliness and Catliness.

3) Be soft and judicious with your speech. Less wording and more purring is often the best approach to life's challenges.

4) Be fully confident in who you are. Know that you are a blessing to the world whether everyone knows it or not.

5) Always view the world from a place of prominence - preferably with a soft pillow and a ball of yarn.

Recently, I gave a sermon on contemporary Universalism mainly because this church was originally a Universalist church before its members chose to join the Unitarian Universalist Association. Today, I will balance out that discussion by offering a similar look at contemporary Unitarianism. Both Unitarianism and Universalism offer our movement unique perspectives that can complement each other and be strong pillars to our understanding of spirituality. They both, however, have some unique characteristics that make them distinct. You might think of the two ideologies as similar to the difference between dogs and cats. The Unitarians are like cats in that they prefer to sit and ponder the great mystery of the one-ness of all things while the Universalists are the canines who love everyone and just want to go out and play. Today we will observe the feline side of our tradition - contemporary Unitarianism.

The Unitarianism that led to the development of the Unitarian church in America began as one of many interpretations of the Christian Reformation movement of the 1500s. In reality, the idea that Jesus is a sacred prophet but not a divine being has been around since his stories first came to light. It's just that those ideas were considered heretical in the orthodoxy that eventually developed in the Christian church. It took the Reformation Movement to bring those ideas back into the light.

One of the fundamental principles of Judaism as it developed in the land of Israel was an insistence on the belief of a single all-encompassing God. One of the most important Jewish prayers, known as the Shema, begins with the words "Hear, O Israel: God is our Lord, God is one." This was a radical departure from the polytheistic practices of many of the cultures the Hebrews encountered or were subjugated to in their history. This monotheism was the paramount religious issue for them.

So, when Christianity developed from Judaism, it began with similar foundations. The concept of the Trinity, or one god in three persons: father, son, and holy spirit, did not fully take hold in Christianity until more than three hundred years after the appearance of Jesus and well after the books of the Bible were collected and canonized. Unitarians and other dissenters pointed out that there is no specific mention of the Trinity anywhere in the Bible - not in either the old testament or the new! How did such a curious, non-Jewish concept become such an important part of the Christian tradition? To answer this we must turn to the legacy of a mighty conqueror from Greece.

When I first came to Boston I remember being overwhelmed by its grandeur and its beauty. I would often be in awe at the sights and sounds of its tall buildings, beautiful art works, incredible music, exciting sports teams, and the range of incredible thought and creativity of its people. Boston is the home, after all, of

Harvard University, MIT, Boston University, and a host of other small but distinctive colleges as well as great art galleries, music venues, theaters and other opportunities for creative and intellectual expression. This same sense of astonishment and reverence must have overcome the visitor of the ancient city of Alexandria in Egypt.

The city was named after Alexander the Great who, after conquering much of the region, wanted to build a living tribute that would extol his greatness. Alexandria became the region's center for intellectuals, artists, and philosophers much like cities such as Boston are today. There, people traded goods and exchanged art and literature but, most of all, they shared ideas. When Christianity reached Alexandria it came across a variety of philosophical ideas. One such theological school known as the neo-Platonists emerged. It was so named because their students studied the works of the Greek philosophers such as Aristotle and Plato. Their goal was to syncretize Christian and Greek thought. Aristotle, after all, had been Alexander the Great's teacher. Aristotle once reportedly wrote, "All things are three, and thrice is all: for as the Pythagoreans say, everything and all things are bound by threes, for the end, and the middle, and the beginning have this number in everything." The Neo-Platonists were a direct influence on the concept of the holy trinity in early Christianity.

There was, of course, much debate about this new trinitarian conceptualization of Christianity but much of it was put to rest by the emperor Constantine and the two councils he called forth in 325 and 451 to end the debate. The concept of the three-in-one that is now so central to Christianity became official church doctrine.

There were some, however, who rejected that doctrine since it was not supported by scripture and because it seemed to suggest the impossible division of an indivisible God. Those who became known later as Unitarians came from Poland and then Romania where the so-called Polish Brethren were forced out of their homeland. Many escaped to Transylvania and Holland because these were two places were differences in Christian theology were tolerated. The acceptance of non-Trinitarians in these lands and other places allowed Unitarian ideals to be discreetly spread through Europe. In the 1700s, Unitarian congregations eventually formed in England. From England, Unitarian ideals sailed to Boston and King's Chapel, in the heart of the city, became the first Unitarian church in America.

Just as in the historical development of the Universalists, by the end of the 18th century and beyond, other theological reforms took place in the ranks of the Unitarians. Through the influence of the Transcendentalists, the Humanists, and exposure to other religious traditions, the Unitarians slowly moved away from their Christian roots. By the time they merged with the Universalists in 1961, they had been transformed into the Post-Christian Unitarian Universalist tradition we have today.

The question for us, then, is how can we develop a contemporary form of Unitarianism that reflects our current range of theological stances - if we can even claim one at all? I believe we can. I believe we can concur on the word "unity" which is the foundation of the word Unitarian. Regardless of religion, spiritual practice, or even in the absence of any professed religious belief, I think we can all agree that we are each and every one of us intimately connected to this one reality, this one earth, and this one universe in which we exist. Even if there are multiple universes, it is this one universe to which all are experiences, our actions, and our hopes are bound. Whether we wish to acknowledge it or not, we are intimately connected and interconnected to each other. Like flicking a single strand in the web of a spider, what one does in a single place and time reverberates to all.

But, declaring a one-ness of existence is not enough for a truly religious viewpoint unless we can claim a connection to this unity. We find that relationship through something enigmatic, mystifying, and awe-inspiring about our existence together. That mystery is the source of this living, creative, and transformative universe into whose celestial luminous fabric we find ourselves thoroughly enmeshed. We cannot deny that there is a force (or Spirit of Life, if you will) within us that moves us forward in motion and that even those things we call inanimate are also surrounded by motion and growth. All things from bacteria to galaxies are part of one great enthralling universal dance of constant renewal and awakening. All things are enlivened and enriched by what has been sometimes called the "ghost in the machine".

The term "ghost in the machine" has been used to point out the mistake in the concept of a separate mind-body duality. If mind, or spirit, is separate from the physical body (as dualists claim), then you must have a separate, non-physical entity within to control it. That is the ghost in the machine. The idea is that a ghost in the machine points out the flaw in the claim of separate duality.

To illustrate the concept of the ghost in the machine, I wanted to bring you something more aesthetic than a machine - something much cuter. So, I present the ghost in the Pusheen. If you don't know, Pusheen is a famous internet icon popular with a lot of screen intensive children. You have to admit she's infinitely cuter than any kind of machine. You might also note that she has no ghost within her anymore than there is one inside me or any of you. Though she is not alive, Pusheen is full of billions of molecules and electrons and particles all of which are in motion and in relationship with each other. The only difference is that we possess independent control of our own fiefdom of molecules.

The breathtaking realization of this constantly creative and emerging unity of energy and transfiguration is almost incomprehensible to us. It is the great mystery. It is the source of awe and wonder that is the core of all religions. This essential interdependent unity through mystery is made manifest in all the beauty and enchantment of the natural world. It is the single sacred unity through which we can identify as contemporary Unitarians. It is the very one-ness that mystics of all religious traditions speak.

When we are unable to recognize the contemporary Unitarian concept of sacred and interdependent one-ness then we become part of the "me" generation. Let us look at the great mystery of the interdependent web of which we are a part and seek the wisdom of the cat. It is then that we will learn to become the "meow" generation.

Notes

1. Pusheen the Cat can be found at Pusheen.com
2. The Ghost in the Machine by Arthur Koestler

Sermon 8

For The Love of Cookies: The Meaning of Equity

Series: Soul Matters Themes

Delivered on February 11, 2024

Introduction

This is one of several sermons with topics based on monthly themes suggested by a UU group known as Soul Matters. I would sometimes lead off the first sermon of the month with a sermon based on that month's suggested theme. The topic for the month of February was "equity". I wanted to address how traditional religion in many Western countries has moved from its roots in liberation to a justification for the proliferation of wealth. I wanted to encourage us to support others by serving rather than saving.

The Sermon

Have you ever heard anyone say that something is 'awfully good'? How is that possible? Either something is awful or it's good. How can it be both? How about the phrase 'crash landing'? I think it's safe to say that if you crash something into the ground that you didn't really land it. Here's another one: 'seriously funny'. How can something be funny if you're being serious about it? My daughter knows I am serious about my great Dad jokes but she's never said I was seriously funny. Come to think of it, she's never said my Dad jokes were funny at all. Now that's pretty serious.

Those kinds of phrases are known as oxymorons and here's a few more examples: a civil war, jumbo shrimp, governmental organization, express mail, peacekeeper missile.

Here's one more for you: nutritional cookie! How can there be a dessert that's nutritional? Is there such a thing? It turns out there is. Nutritional cookies are round wafers full of protein, grains, and vitamins. Hold on to that fact for just a short minute because we're going to need those awfully good nutritional cookies later on before they become old news.

The theme for this month's services is Justice and Equity. I want to focus today on the concept of equity. Most people understand the term equality but may not be as familiar with the concept of equity. They are not the same thing and the difference is subtle but very important. Equality is based on the mathematical term "equal" which means the 'the same as'. One plus two equals–or is the same as–three. To treat people with equality means to treat them all the same way. As Universalists, we can appreciate the value of equality since we believe that all people deserve to be treated with equal worth and dignity. Sometimes, though, equality is not enough to reach a true state of fairness and justice. Sometimes people need equity, instead.

To understand the difference between equality and equity I'm going to bring back the nutritional cookie and I apologize but we're going to have to do a little math here. Imagine there are three people looking for these nutritional cookies and we happen to have fifteen to offer them. Applying equality would dictate that we give each person five cookies. That seems fair, right? But, what if we spent a little time talking to all three of these folks and found out that Person 1 has just eaten dinner, Person 2 hasn't eaten since breakfast, and Person 3 hasn't had a decent meal in several days. Might that information change how we distribute our nutri-snacks? It would be equitable for us to offer more to Person 3 than we do for Person 2 who, in turn, would get more than Person 1. Equity is more challenging than equality because it involves taking the time to understand what each person actually needs.

Equality does not always mean fairness because not all people begin in the same place, under the same conditions, or with the same opportunities.

So now we know what equity is but what does equity look like? Unfortunately, the very country that should be the symbol of human equity is not. That is because America, despite its constitution and its stand for democracy, is not a very equitable nation. According to Forbes Magazine, the top 10% of the country's population owns 70% of the total wealth. That's a lot of cookies in just a few hands. Many countries in Europe, the Pacific, and elsewhere offer free universal health care, free access to college, a livable minimum wage, have tough environmental restrictions, and have progressive taxation–all of which have been proven over time to provide greater equity and happiness, I might add, to their populations. Most of the Scandinavian countries who have many social support networks for all their citizens also consistently rate high on degrees of happiness. America, however, has fiercely resisted all these things.

Why? Why has the country that fought so hard for freedom from tyranny and unfair taxation now become one of the richest but most inequitable countries in the world? One reason is because justice and equity are rooted in love. You have to care deeply in your heart about the lives of all people in order to be motivated to work for a truly equitable society. I'm afraid that this country lacks that empathy and I believe a large part of the blame for this condition must be placed on the very institution that is supposed to teach and spread compassion–the church. People don't talk about this but what better place and time to point out this reality than in a church around Valentine's day? Despite its rhetoric I think the history of the church in Europe and America has done much to promote class consciousness and division. Let me explain.

First, let me say that I am not talking about any of the thousands of religious leaders and laity of all religions of compassion who have worked tirelessly and with great conviction to help other people live better lives. I am talking about mostly political leaders who have used religion to further their goals of power and control.

The first was the emperor Constantine in the fourth century who was not himself a Christian but made Christianity the official religion of the Roman Empire. His mother was Christian and is often credited with turning him toward her faith but I think it was more likely that he saw how rapidly Christianity was spreading throughout the empire. Early Christianity appealed to the poor and the oppressed of which there were many in the vast Roman empire. Secondly, since Jesus had died for them, early Christians were willing to die for him. I think Constantine may have admired that conviction and its appeal to many in his empire. For whatever reason, Constantine made Christianity the official religion of the Roman Empire even though he was never baptized himself until the day of his death.

The result of his action meant that Christianity, the religion of the poor, of the destitute, of the persecuted, became the religion of the conqueror, the oppressor, and the colonizer. The drive for the expansion of the Roman empire took place not just for the glory of Rome but for the glory of God as well. Domination of other cultures became a God-given right because the dominated were not humans but subhumans, the heathen, the people who needed to be conquered, controlled, and converted. Even after the Roman empire crumbled away, the church continued to develop and maintain power throughout the world. Even kings and queens had to be confirmed by the church in order to be considered legitimate.

This domination continued for almost a thousand years–a thousand(!)–until it was challenged by the Reformation in the 1500s and the thinkers of the Enlightenment in the 1600s. By the time the United States of America was underway there was a movement to create a country not ruled either by aristocracy or theocracy. The result was freedom and democracy–but only for the white males. Non-Christians were still considered heathens and subhuman. It became the country's manifest destiny to conquer, control, and convert the heathens of all lands whether they were Natives, Africans, Chinese, or anyone considered non-American.

Our country was built on a slave economy and even though slavery officially ended with the Emancipation Proclamation, a form of slave economy still continues today. Large groups of people continue to be paid wages within or below the poverty line and are alienated from the products they produce. Those who have money and power believe they deserve what they have but feel those less fortunate do not. Some even go so far as to say that their wealth is a sign of their approval from God. They believe that the rich. Therefore, it is the sacred duty of the powerful and rich to fight against every effort to change the system toward greater equity.

We do not know what equity looks like here because equity must be rooted in love and compassion rather than status and power. Equity can only be based on a belief in the sacred worth of all people from all religions. Churches like ours who embrace the moral principles of Universalism can help nudge the country towards equity. As much as it was the duty of the past to conquer, control, and convert it is our duty now to upend, uphold, and uplift by encouraging equity, equality, and egalitarianism for all.

This may seem like a daunting task but I want to mention three spiritual tools that I believe can help us walk this path and they are: to listen, to serve, and to get involved. Just as with our nutritional cookies, equity begins by listening to people, to hear their stories, to find out what they need. When we find out what others require we can then begin to serve rather than save. We can learn what needs to be done from those who know how to do it. Lastly, we can work to get involved in changing the system. Power and wealth will always coagulate. Neither will ever be freely distributed without pressure and in our society pressure comes from fairness in legislation. As long as this country remains a free democracy, we can affect change through legal means but only if we get involved in the process. Equity begins in love and love begins in us.

Notes

1. "How can we make it right? What the world's religions have to say about justice: From a Buddhist to a humanist, seven faith leaders weigh in on building a better world" by Carol Kuruvilla

https://www.vox.com/the-highlight/22419487/religion-justice-fairness

2. "The Fairest of them all: Why Europe beats the US on Equality" by Lucas Chancel

https://www.theguardian.com/commentisfree/2018/jan/24/fairest-europeans-inequality-surged-us-europe

3. *Constantine: Roman Emperor, Christian Victor* by Paul Stephenson

Sermon 9

It's What's Hot: The Spirit of Chili

Series: Special Days
Delivered February 25, 2024

Introduction

After having arrived at the Barre Church I carried on a personal tradition of having chili festivals at my home. Moving into an apartment made it less possible for me to continue that tradition so I decided to bring it to the church. We started a chili festival in the Winter that focused on a chili cooking contest that attracted both local chefs and home enthusiasts.

The chili festival was held on a Sunday afternoon so I challenged myself to write a sermon for that morning centered on chili itself. The multiple flavors and styles combined together to make one tasty dish reminded me of the strength of Universalism.

The Sermon

I often put quite a bit of research time into the preparation of my sermons and every once in a while I run across something interesting. As it happened, I came upon a video with a title that stated "You Can Preach About Anything." It was a very clever video. In it, people walked around a room, picked up random objects, and then started to speak about how that object represented something spiritual. It was quite ingenious and it got me thinking. Could I possibly write a sermon about something as ordinary as a bowl of chili? I don't mean just a speech about the history and make-up of chili, but a purposeful sermon about the meaning of chili itself? I mean, I know you expect me to speak eloquently about compassion or pontificate about good moral judgment or give the old 'hope at the end of a rope' homily–but would you expect me to deliver a sermon about a bowl of hot peppers? I thought it might be fun to try. Besides, for me, chili is something very special.

In seminary we are taught to give sermons about the things that are important to us. We speak about subjects in which we may have a personal experience or elucidate topics upon things that reach our own souls. We are taught to share our own stories and to speak about what we know and love. Chili has all those qualifications for me; it holds a special place in my heart. It has a particular significance to me that I thought might turn a simple bowl of beans into a relevant message for all of us as it did for me. But, how can a simple meal be so meaningful? How can a spicy soup be a lifesaver?

First, let's get to know our subject at hand through the main ingredient of chili: the rather innocent looking chili pepper. It is small and colorful but, as we all know, can pack a punch way above its weight class. That is because all peppers have different levels of a compound called capsaicin which acts upon the receptors in our bodies that alert us to the presence of dangerous heat. They trick those receptors into sending a burn warning through our bodies even though there is no actual physical burning.

The degree of that searing sensation is measured in what are called Scoville Heat Units, or SHUs, named after its inventor the pharmacist William Scoville. SHUs determine the number of times the capsaicin in a particular pepper needs to be diluted before it is no longer detectable. For example, a bell pepper is rated at 0 SHUs which means 'no heat' while the typical jalapeno pepper can range anywhere from 2500 to 8,000 SHUs. Compare that to the infamous Carolina Reaper Pepper, one of the hottest in the world, which can register on the Scoville Scale at more than 2 million SHUs. The chili pepper, of course, evolved into such a potent plant because it uses capsaicin as a means of protection against creatures who might consume it and not as a way to shock and delight our palette. But, as it turns out, people have been enjoying its unique flavor for thousands of years.

Chili means many things to many people. Its powerful heat effect became a talisman to ward off evil for some. For others it was a natural tool to help predict the future, to bring good luck, to bring rain, and to aid digestion. Chilis were burned to fumigate houses and were even worn as protective amulets. There is even a religious group dedicated to the worship of all things chili called the Transcendental Capsaiciniphillic Society.

The chili pepper was first cultivated by humans in the land we now call Bolivia in South America in 7500 BC. To the Incas, the chili was a sacred plant. The Aztecs used the plant as a form of currency. In some cultures in Central America, chili was mixed with tobacco to create a potent hallucinogenic potion that aided shamans in their journeys to the spirit world. The American Hopi people celebrate a sacred day at this time of year called Powamu which is when the kachinas or sacred spirits, often honored in the making of ceremonial dolls, descend from their mountain homes to bring the people good health and fortune. One of those is the chili kachina named Tsil who encourages people to run fast or risk the possibility of having their mouth stuffed with hot chili peppers.

From South America and Mexico, the chili pepper made its way to Texas where it became an important staple in feeding cowboys in the midst of long cattle drives. It is interesting to note here that meat was considered too valuable a commodity to be added to their chili so beans were added as a protein instead. The popularity of chili soon spread and became an important meal in

Texas. Chili stands were set up in every town in the state but the best chili was to be found in the jails, each of which competed to have the best chili. The chili of Texas eventually became so popular that it soon crossed state borders. In 1893, chili was introduced at the Chicago World's Fair where it quickly spread throughout the rest of the country and became an inexpensive staple of the American diet.

This nationwide popularity for a bowl of chili inevitably led to the development of culinary factions, each of whom claimed to know the "correct" way to prepare the spicy dish. There are those who claim that a chili dish should have no meat while others claim that it should contain no beans. Some insist on no ground beef while others dismiss the use of any fillers such as rice or pasta. Over the years people have experimented by adding beer, chocolate, bacon, coffee, chickpeas, coconut, you name it. If you can imagine it, someone has probably tried it – much to the horror of chili purists.

To me, a great bowl of chili should seize upon all your senses at once. It should offer a total experience. It should have a wonderfully complex and integrated taste. The heat of the chili peppers should not be overwhelming as that can destroy the experience of other flavors but it should be enough to snap our attention back into the present moment. Chili is about mindfulness. As you place it on your tongue you are brought directly into the present moment. You experience all the flavor sensations at once: sweet, savory, salty, sour, bitter, and, yes, hot.

You will also encounter a range of textures through the meats, the vegetables, the chilis, the sauce, the beans, or whatever else that may be found within the meal. Most of all, those ingredients should be balanced in such a way that none overtakes the other. That should also be the way of a strong and vibrant multicultural society. Just as with a peaceful society of different people, chili is about the many in the one and the one in the many. Chili is a visual and culinary symbol of the strength of unity in diversity. Chili is a symbol of the deliciousness of diversity.

Consider how a great chili chef might gather a variety of food and flavor elements and consider how each adds to the desired outcome. Individual shapes, flavors, and textures are combined into something that, if well done, will be a novel amalgamation of flavors. The result should be something more complex, more meaningful, and more wonderful than the original constituents. Yet, those combined ingredients will still retain some of their own unique flavor identities. A great congregation is like a great bowl of chili. Each of you is a wonderful and unique flavor with your own strengths and weaknesses but here, in this place, we combine these ingredients to build something stronger, more wonderful, more–dare I say–divine. This is what chili can mean to us.

Chili has always had a special meaning to me as well. Like many people, I struggle mightily in the midst of the Winter. When the sunlight is sparse, the days are cold, the winds bite through me, and I feel trapped inside. I can get a heavy case of the Winter Blues. Every September I dread the thought of the approach of Winter and so I depend a lot on the seasonal holidays to get me through. But, after New Year's Day, the holiday landscape is as barren as the cold and snowy terrain outside my frosted window. President's Day isn't the same and, since my divorce, Valentine's Day just doesn't do it for me anymore. The year may be new but the full onslaught of Winter makes me feel old, tired, and empty.

To overcome that slip into sorrow I decided many years ago that I needed another holiday – something in late February that I could look forward to. I needed something full of fun and frolic and called for great food and friendship. Something that would snap my senses into the present and fire up my soul to carry me forward into the Springtime. That something became a chili festival and it would be my hope at the end of the rope.

Notes

1. "The Trail of Fire: The Story of the Chili Pepper" by Christopher Patrick Kelly.

https://synapticspace.wordpress.com/2019/05/02/the-long-journey-of-the-chili-pepper/

2. Chili Peppers in Legend and Lore
https://www.fieryfoodscentral.com/2008/07/02/chile-peppers-in-legend-and-lore/

3. "The Chili Pepper: History's Hot Pepper" by Candace Hunter.

https://thepracticalherbalist.com/advanced-herbalism/chili-pepper-historys-hot-pepper/

4. The Transcendental Capsaicinophilic Society

http://www.chetbacon.com/tcs/tcs.html

Sermon 10

The Soul-Ar Eclipse

Series: Special Days

Delivered April 7, 2024

Introduction

I was lucky enough to be in Vermont during a full solar eclipse that took place on April 8. Barre was on the inside edge of the path of the total eclipse which meant that we would see the full eclipse for about ten minutes. People from all around New England drove hours to places within Vermont that would experience the eclipse. Barre itself was overwhelmed with people making the event the single-most important astrological as well as economic occasion for the area.

What surprised and disturbed me the most was the fact that people were still willing to use the event to spread fear and division through outrageous predictions of the end of the world. I turned my attention, instead, toward the phenomenal beauty of the event and what it could teach us.

The Sermon

Imagine, if you will. You are on a wide open plain with your extended family. You are hunting. It could be for buffalo, or deer, or bear, or moose or you might be fishing. All you know is that if you do not find and catch your prey that your family will go hungry. You have only simple weapons and your own wisdom and experience to guide you. There are no vehicles, no fancy weapons, no electricity, no lights, no buildings to hide within if the weather turns rough. There is only you, your family, the animals, the land, a wide open sky, and the brilliance and warmth of a bright burning sun.

But then, as you continue the hunt, you begin to notice some very strange and frightening things happening around you. The bright greens of the trees, the browns of the hills, the deep blue of the sky, and the other colors around begin to dull into varied shades of gray. The shadows on the trees start to move–not imperceptibly slow like they do throughout the day–but they seem to be almost creeping on the ground. New and strange whiskery shadows appear on the ground as well. Then, there's a glow on the horizon like there is at the end of the day but the glow is not in just one spot. It surrounds you in all directions yet it is the middle of the day. Soon after, the skies grow dark–almost as dark as night. The sun disappears but there is no moonlight. Everything is suddenly draped in the gloomy cover of an early dusk. Something has taken the sun away. You think to yourself: this must be the end of the world.

It is not the end of the world, of course. It is a total solar eclipse but such events have always been very frightening and disturbing for people who did not understand what was actually happening in the sky above them. In ancient Mesopotamia, solar eclipses were taken as a sign that the death of their king was imminent. In 585 BC, the Greek city-states of Lydia and Media suddenly ended their six-year war and negotiated with each other for peace when they found themselves in the midst of a total solar eclipse. In 1133, the death of England's King Henry I coincided with a solar eclipse. The English were so frightened about the meaning of that event that the whole country was thrown into a civil war.

But, in case you thought that such superstitious fears of the eclipse are relegated only to the past, consider the multiple postings of people who have claimed that the total solar eclipse of 2017 was the cause of larger than normal hurricanes, unusual solar flares, and multiple earthquakes. There was, of course, absolutely no scientific evidence given for any of these claims. Even now, in 2024, according to one website, the solar eclipse is expected to bring on the beginning of World War Three and the destruction of New York City, Baltimore, Washington DC, and Boston. I am thankful, therefore, that I will be here in Vermont for the event rather than back in Boston.

Much of this fear, of course, is due to the fact that people did not understand what was happening in the sky and why. Being the rational creatures that we are, we tend to invent answers when we don't have any answers. For many cultures, the eclipse looked to them as if the sun was being devoured by another creature such as a frog, wolf, or enormous dragon. In order to prevent that from happening people shouted and made loud noises to try and warn the sun. Some shot flaming arrows into the sky to try and reignite the burning star. Others thought the sun and moon were fighting or that they were lovers and just wanted a few moments of privacy. For other cultures, the disappearance of the sun was a clear sign that their god or gods were angry and wanted to send a dire warning. The eclipse has been the focus for a great many sacrifices, repentances, revivals, prayers, and rituals and, for better or worse, the incantations and supplications worked because the light of the sun always returned.

In order to prepare for our own upcoming celestial event we need to understand exactly what actually happens up in the sky during a solar eclipse. First of all, without using an inordinate amount of scientific verbiage and complicated language, let me explain in the simplest terms possible what exactly happens to the sun during a total solar eclipse… Nothing! That's right, nothing. No disappearance, no devouring, no pitched battles, no mysterious acts of disappearance–nothing. But, what happens to the moon during a total solar eclipse as it dares to cross the path of the mighty sun? Well… nothing! Again, nothing–no munching, no crunching, and no punching–nothing. The only thing that does happen is that the shadow of our moon caused by the light of our sun crosses over certain portions of the earth's surface as the moon passes overhead.

The only reason we experience this event is that our own planetary hitchhiker, the moon, is close enough and large enough to bear upon us its own shadow, or umbra, as the scientists call it, in the same way that an umbrella is able to block out the light of the sun. Even though the sun is 400 times the size of the moon and the fact that it is 400 times as far from the earth than the moon means that even a small planetary satellite, like ours, can create a fairly large shadow on its host. But I want to emphasize that nothing has ever been destroyed by a shadow.

There is, however, one thing that does experience significant changes during a solar eclipse and that one thing is, well, us. Beings on earth depend on the cycles of the moon and the sun to regulate biological rhythms. Besides, we really like our patterns, our habits, and our routines. We like it when familiar things appear as expected. That is the magic of the recurrence of Santa Claus, the Easter Bunny, and Dr. Who. A sudden disruption of cycles, however, can create fear and panic and a total solar eclipse can feel frightening. It has been noted that people actually do experience changes in pulse rate, heart rate, perspiration, and breathing during an eclipse and there are the very real dangers of eye damage caused from looking up at the event with the naked eyes. Another recorded effect of past eclipses is the scores of terrible car crashes that happen.

I remember when my daughter and I used to watch a show together where a professional magician in a mask performed a difficult magic trick and then revealed how the trick was done. We loved that show but I couldn't help thinking that pulling the curtain away from the conjuring would take away from the excitement and thrill of watching magic shows in the same way that I have just debunked the folklore of eclipses here. I was wrong about the magic show because knowing how the trick was done just made us appreciate the artistry of the magician even more. There may not have been any true magic but there was plenty of mastery and majesty.

The same can be said for grand celestial events such as a total solar eclipse. There may not be any magic involved but there will still be a lot of beauty, grandeur, and splendor. We will be reminded–if only for a brief time–of the incredible wonders beyond our own planet. Through a sudden alteration of the routine patterns of our day we will be awakened to the significance of the sun in our lives and to the lives of every being on this earth. We will be captured by the absence of its brilliance while caught up in a mix of bewilderment, dread, and disorientation, perhaps. And, finally, we will be swept into a state of awe and wonder.

The feeling of being peripheral in the midst of a mighty and majestic and unbelievably enormous and constantly evolving universe can be disconcerting at best but it can also be the source of a feeling of deep reverence. This sense of wonder, fascination, and admiration of something much bigger than ourselves is the source and seed of every religious tradition both old and new. We see these amazing things and then we ask why and how. Our answers to those questions become our systems of belief.

I think, however, there is yet another lesson we may learn from the solar eclipse. During the impending darkness we may experience unexpected losses: of light, of heat, of time, of routine, and maybe even of identity. It is said that sometimes we do not appreciate the things we have until they are gone. As the light of the sun is swept away by the silent shadow of the moon, let it remind us that our lives here are transitory and that all things will change, sometimes in anticipated ways, but sometimes in shockingly unexpected ways. Let it remind us that at any time in our lives the things we have come to depend upon can be swept away in the breadth of a whisper or the space of a tragedy. Let us surrender to the moment and to the experience as it may teach us about gratitude and reciprocity and compassion for others. Let it remind us to emit our light as bright as we can but to also accept the darker moments and help others find their time to shine.

Finally, let it remind us of the futility of our own actions. We are here for but a short time on this planet and yet we spend most of that time fighting, squabbling, and arguing with each other while our brief lights are ignited and then snuffed out. The sun and the moon do not fight, they do not possess, and they do not seek to control. They exist in their own realms–simply and majestically–in peace and fulfillment. I believe we can learn those lessons for ourselves as we watch those heavenly bodies dance in the sky together.

Notes

1. "How chasing solar eclipses opened me up to the awe of living" by Kate Russo.

https://aeon.co/ideas/how-chasing-solar-eclipses-opened-me-up-to-the-awe-of-living

2. "American Indian Beliefs About the eclipse" by Dennis Zotigh

https://www.smithsonianmag.com/blogs/national-museum-american-indian/2017/08/21/american-indian-beliefs-about-eclipse/

Sermon 11

The Myth of the Straight Line

Series: The Emergence of God

Delivered on April 21, 2024

Introduction

If there is one thing that I could hope to change in people it would be the tendency to separate people into different categories. We use the image of a line to make distinctions between things but a straight line is a human concept rarely, if ever, found in nature. The history of humanity is rife with struggles to dominate one group over another for differences that are insignificant and petty. Wars and conflicts are often fought over those who try to identify others as "less than".

The Sermon

There was once a man who could only walk in straight lines. It was terribly challenging for him because he kept bumping into things. He would go straight ahead and then "bam" smack into something before he could turn. You can imagine that he found walking around town to be challenging. Finally, he sought relief and went to his doctor. He said, "Doctor, you've got to help me. I'm only able to walk in a straight line. I keep running into things and I get stuck. Can you help me?" "Of course," replied the doctor. "I can give you a prescription for a drug called cyclobendalot." "Cyclo bendo what?" asked the straight shooter. "Cyclobendalot," returned the confident doctor. "It will have you going in circles in no time." "Then, I'll take it," said the patient. A few weeks later the doctor saw her patient and asked him how he was doing. "Great," replied the patient. "That medicine has done wonders," He said. "I feel like I've finally turned a corner."

We humans love straight lines. We think they make our lives easier. How many times have you heard it said that "the shortest distance between two points is a straight line?" or "An object in motion tends to remain in motion along a straight line." We expect lines to be able to predict where things will go. We expect them to help make things predictable. We expect them to make our lives easier. But, most lives are messy and often follow along wavy arcs that could never have been seen or predicted. Our lives, like many other things, do not follow a straight line.

When I was a young child I wanted to be a psychologist because I wanted to understand people but when I went to visit a psychologist in my neighborhood and he told me that all he did was wake up in the middle of the night to answer desperate phone calls, I changed my mind. One day my parents gave me a trumpet and, much to my parents' dismay, I loved to play it–loudly! I decided then that music was going to be my life. But, all through college when I was not practicing my horn or writing music I was studying religion and after more than twenty years as a professor of music, I realized I wanted to study for the ministry. Now, here I am. Life rarely moves in clear and straight lines.

There is this terrible story we tell our teenagers which says, basically, that if you go to college, choose a career, get a good job, buy a house, and raise a family, you will live happily ever after. This story makes it sound like our path in life is a clear straight line and that happiness is guaranteed at the end of the road but rarely do our lives take such a direct route. The reason for that is that there is no such thing as an absolute straight line. Our lives are more like the path of a pinball as it bounces and rolls its way home. The reality is that straight lines are two-dimensional human constructs imposed on a three-dimensional world. Yet, lines appear everywhere.

Just look around you. The walls here reach straight toward the ceiling which is flat and even. The chairs you sit in are arranged in straight rows. The hymnals you sing from have straight lines on both the outside and the inside. As you look up at me here you see I am surrounded by straight lines: the pulpit, the computer, the table. If you walk out of the building you are in, you can see more straight lines. There are lines painted on the road. There are chimneys, doorways, and windows. There are long and tall poles, electrical cables, phone towers; and signs–lots of geometrically shaped signs–with all kinds of significant lines painted upon them. But, did you notice something about all those lines I just mentioned? They are all from human-made objects.

The British architect William Kent, who is said to be the originator of the home garden, once said that nature abhors a straight line. Nature, of course, doesn't actually abhor anything but it is clear that straight lines are not natural. We may claim to see straight lines in nature such as when we look at the earth's horizon or at the surface of a crystal but usually those things are part of an illusion. The horizon we see at the ocean or across a prairie sky is actually a very tiny part of a very large circle and though the molecules of a crystal look like they line up together, those lines are usually fractured and uneven and the molecules that make up that crystal have no straight lines themselves. Nature abounds in curves, spirals, and fractals, not in straight lines, and the reason for this fact is that curvilinear shapes allow for growth, expansion, and creativity while straight lines do not.

Take a look at this piece of art, for example.

Notice in this work that the natural elements: the sky, the land, and the river are all based on curved lines while the man made elements: the bridge, the railing, and the buildings all are painted with straight lines.

Lines are used to make clear and distinct separations. Lines make divisions. Lines imply direct cause and effect. Lines force us to choose between "this" and "that" but nature doesn't work that way. Everything in nature is made up of gradual progressions and spectrums of evolution. You can find many examples of things that seem to be in opposition but are really just the endpoints of a process of change. When exactly does day become night? When it's completely dark? Is the night sky ever completely dark? When exactly does someone become old? My daughter says I am old but my retired friends at my favorite coffee shop say I am young. Where does the mind end and the body begin? Do you really think my mind cannot influence my body or that my body does not affect my mind? There are no clear lines between these things. How you define any of these polarities depends on their relationship to whatever you are comparing them. Lines create the appearance of separate but false dyads. Day and night, young and old, and mind and body are just a few of the many things we try to divide but which are, in reality, just opposite points within a long continuum. Here is another example: science and religion.

There have been many heated battles between scientists and theologians claiming that each knows the truth but it is possible that the truth is both religious and scientific. Both have value and significance. Science can help us bring safe and nutritious food to our tables but it cannot add significance to that meal in the same way that a seder, the Eucharist, the end of Ramadan, or a Sunday family dinner does. Science teaches us about life while religion teaches us how to live. Science and religion are not binary dyads separated by a clear straight line. They are more like two points that hold up either side of a cosmic hammock with lots of intertwining strings between them.

The straight line we impose in our thinking can cause us a lot of trouble because it creates division where separation might not actually exist. Lines can also create square boxes in which we can throw things and categorize them. Boxes can then be moved and stacked so that some things become higher or take on greater significance than others. Boxes create false classifications that may be convenient for labeling but which do not reflect reality. Consider all the packaged labels we add to such things as gender, sexuality, religious perspective, race, class, political affiliation, and on and on. All of these things fall within a spectrum of possibilities yet we insist in locking people into one definitive box or another. Gender, for example, exists on a spectrum. People experience their own gender in a complex variety of ways and those ways can be expressed in a complex variety of relationships. We know that years of trying to force that spectrum of sexuality and gender into two distinct boxes has caused harm and suffering. The same can be said for race and class. The distinctions and labels made in each of these areas are designed to separate and prioritize one classification over another and in each case those hierarchical divisions are false.

All of the universe is a whole but within that whole everything is constantly becoming something else and everything contains a little bit of its opposite within it. That is the yin and yang of things. Nothing is purely one thing, classifications are false, and straight lines are an illusion. We are all wonderfully beautiful evolving squishy blobs of uniqueness swirling about in an even greater and more beautiful blob of creative wonder. We are each slithering through fascinating and challenging curvilinear pathways forward. I hope you enjoy the journey.

Notes

1. The painting is The Scream by Edvard Munch

2. William Kent was an 18th century architect and landscape architect. He also painted and designed furniture.

Sermon 12

An Or-Dune-Ary Day

Series: Special Days

Delivered on May 5, 2024

Introduction

The Barre UU Church ordained me as a Universalist (UU) minister on May 5, 2024 in the afternoon. That morning we had a regular service and I gave a sermon on what I thought ordination meant for a UU church. In the pews were members of the Barre UU church as well as members of the Stow, Massachusetts church and long-time friends who did so much to emotionally support me through seminary. By the end of the ceremony I was so emotional with joy and disbelief that I had made it to that point that I openly wept.

The Sermon

We are told that a sermon should open with a joke–something funny and light-hearted that will lift the spirits of the congregation and focus their attention on the speaker's supposedly brilliant orations. I was going to begin this sermon by discussing the spiritual lessons of the movie Dune, the recently released blockbuster science fiction film series about the struggles of the people living on the desert planet of Arrakis, but I was told that my humor was just too dry, that I needed to water it down a bit, that it might be too gritty for a refined audience such as yourselves.

The Dune series of novels, written by Frank Herbert, has had several attempts at movie adaption. Most of these have failed, I believe, for primarily two reasons: 1) The original Dune books were written mostly in dialogue and I don't mean the inconsequential coffee and croissant kind of banter. The conversations in the books are paranoid, pointed, cryptic, and laced with meanings. Most popular movies today are about action: people fighting, things blowing up, fantastic scenery, more things blowing up, complex battles, romance, and even more things blowing up. 2) Film depictions of Dune up to now have tried to fit the plot into the standard archetypal story about a hero who rises forth from the people and saves them from tyranny and oppression, but that is not what Dune is really about at all. There's a deeper, more intriguing, and cautionary tale and lesson embedded within the Dune series–something to which we should pay attention, something profound about humanity, something that is still highly relevant to our lives today.

But wait, you might say. Today is not about blockbuster movies. It's supposed to be about ordination and you would be right. This congregation of the Barre Unitarian Universalist Church has chosen to ordain me this very afternoon. They have invited me to become a member of the clergy so that I may better serve the needs of this church and of this community. So, let's take a moment to talk about ordination and like many UU sermons, let us begin with a good, dry definition.

The word ordination comes from the Latin word "ordinaire" which literally means "to put in order". Traditionally, the idea was that the ordained were people connected through a succession of priests and prophets from the past to the present. More currently, especially in our UU congregations, ordination has become a formal means of recognizing individuals who take on pastoral functions. Though this path has often involved a series of studies, internships, ministerial reviews, and guided discernments, none of these are absolutely required under the independent polity that is the heart of Unitarian Universalism. Though this allows for a great deal of freedom in practice and application for those a congregation may choose to call minister, it also incurs a weighty responsibility upon those congregations. Our tradition has no pope, no bishops, and no deacons. In effect, a congregation collectively takes on the mantle of the priesthood itself so that it may collectively pass the baton of ministry to one they have chosen.

Ordination is the blessing of one so that one may bless others. It is a seed of sustenance planted by a congregation. It is the formation of an individual for the transformation of a community. It is the recognition of a calling. But what is a calling? In our tradition, we do not believe that you have to be struck down with a bolt of lightning by someone or something from on high. There need not be a burning bush on Facetime or the arrival of an angel in a heavenly Uber. We believe a calling is something that emerges from deep within the heart although I do think the universe has been sending me spiritual text messages throughout my life concerning this path. When I first announced several years ago to my friends–many of whom are sitting in this room right now–that I wanted to pursue the ministry, they responded with a shrug and said, "of course you are!" Evidently, I hadn't been checking my celestial messages.

I've always struggled with the idea of a calling. Not just because it implies that some outside power has to dial your number but because it also implies that someone who is "called" is of more importance than others who are not. I cannot accept this notion. Though ordination may be something that happens to a person, it can never be just about that person. Ordination is not a change in status; it is a change of function. One is ordained for the same reason that pillars are set in temples, pulpits are placed in churches, and candles are lit in altars. Such things provide support, offer a place to focus, and instill hope. Ministers are asked to be pastoral, prophetic, and proclamatory so that they may support a community but it must be kept in mind that they are not the community just as a building alone cannot be a church or the flame of a candle cannot be a prayer.

The role of an ordained clergy person, regardless of faith or tradition, should be focused not on personal goals but on carrying forward the ideals and principles of their tradition in the light of the challenges and conditions of the times. In my case, I have chosen to further the ideals of Unitarian Universalism. Yet, we–as a relatively young tradition– still struggle on defining our ideals.

In previous sermons given here I have proposed that our Unitarian heritage can serve as our theological principle while our Universalist heritage is the foundation of our ethical ambitions. To be a contemporary Unitarian, in my view, is to recognize that all beings are interconnected through one great mystery we may call by many names. Similarly, I believe contemporary Universalism is the way in which we respond to this great sacred enigma with just three basic guidelines. 1) that all people–all beings– inherently deserve respect and dignity, 2) that no one person, tradition, or institution can know the whole truth of the great mystery, and 3) that our lives are enhanced and fulfilled when we grow together in love. These are the beacons I hope to follow on my path that you have lit for me.

The problem with giving prestige, status, or title to any individual is that the power needed to guide or sustain an organization can, in itself, become intoxicating. If not kept in check by other individuals, or more effectively, through some kind of charter, compact, or covenant, one's desire to control and manipulate will grow in the same degree of magnitude as will one's own self image. As many allegories teach us: the cavern of good intentions can also be the lair of the beast.

This is the message of several of the world's greatest science fiction and fantasy stories. In the Lord of the Rings, the one-ring that rules them all also makes the person wearing that ring become invisible like the spirit of the dead– a wraith. Furthermore, the possessor of the ring will give up all family ties and relationships in their sole pursuit of power over others. George Lucas was greatly inspired by the stories of Dune. In his series, Star Wars, young Anakin Skywalker is on the path to becoming a great Jedi Knight but begins to believe that his personal needs and objectives are more important and his view of the world is more accurate than the Jedi Order to whom he has dedicated his life. His internal focus becomes the avenue for the encroachment of the dark side.

The six books of Dune have the same message but it is not an incidental plot line. It is the central focus of the entire series. But, it only becomes evident after the first novel. The main character, Paul Atriedes, is given great power through which he believes he can liberate the desert people of Arrakis and claims himself to be both emperor and messiah so that he can rule unimpeded. He believes it is the only possible way to effect change. In the second book of the series, Paul is asked if there should be a constitution for the new empire. Paul rejects the idea and says, "The constitution is social power mobilized and it has no conscience. It can crush the highest and the lowest, removing all dignity and individuality." But that is just the point. A covenant built upon the highest ideals cannot succumb to ego, power, or conceit. Paul's iron-clad rule and messianic identity becomes the impetus for a holy way where millions are killed or subjugated in his name. The desert people Paul meant to free eventually lose their all-powerful spice they once controlled as they lose their traditional way of life based upon that spice.

So, today I am to be ordained, but the ordination is not about me. It is about you–the people here who have loved and supported me through this effort. It is about this church and its ideals that we hope to bring forward. It is about this community and the hope we have for its future. It is about promoting space for people to live and think freely. It is about our covenant that we share together as a guide and ideal. Most of all, this ordination is about our need to overcome fear with love.

Notes

1. "Becoming a Unitarian Universalist Minister"
https://www.uua.org/careers/ministers/becoming

2. The First Three Dune Books: *Dune* by Frank Herbert, *Dune Messiah* by Frank Herbert, and *Children of Dune* by Frank Herbert.

Sermon 13

The Myth of Design: Traveling Without A Map

Series: The Emergence of God

Delivered on June 2, 2024

Introduction

This sermon continued the series on my book but with more of a personal focus. In it I include three stories that helped to illustrate a rather controversial idea which is that there is unlikely to be a divine plan set out for us from a directorial style deity and the idea of such a plan may actually be oppressive. Along the way I wanted to address the idea of evil as a consequence of choice and not circumstance.

The Sermon

A friend once came to me and said "I'm moving to San Francisco and I need someone to drive my car across the country. I jumped at the opportunity. Instead of taking three to four days to make the journey on a series of interstate highways, however, I decide to drive mostly on state roads and alternative routes so that I might see more of this expansive and amazing country. It took me more than a month to get across.

I kept my eye not just on the road but on the signs that led me to points of interest along the way. I saw the St. Louis Arch, the endless fields of Kansas, the dazzling peaks of the Rocky Mountains, the stunning beauty of the Grand Canyon, the lights of Las Vegas, the starkness of Death Valley, and the mighty waves that crash along the Pacific Coast highway. I also stopped at many small shops and cafes that offered things I had never known before and some that I never want to experience again. All of this was because I had no plan other than to go West. There were many experiences on that trip that I treasure to this day but which I never would have had if I stuck to a straightforward path.

Consider the story of Henry. Henry lost his daughter one day in a mysterious car crash. She went off the road for apparently no reason. She had not been speeding, she had not been drinking or using drugs, there was no one else on the road. The streets were dry and clear. She had somehow just taken a very bad turn. Henry simply could not accept that his beloved child would have died for no reason. He searched for that reason for months on end and what he finally concluded was that he was being punished for not going to church. Now, I'm not going to tell you that bad things can happen if you don't come to church regularly but, hey, why take chances? In any case, Henry became a regular church goer until the day he died.

In 2019, when my life literally fell apart and I tried desperately to make sense of it all, I had lots of well meaning people try to comfort me with phrases such as: 'Everything happens for a reason'; or 'When one door closes, another opens'; or 'It's all part of God's plan'. Those phrases were of no comfort to me and succeeded only in confounding me. I could not imagine saying to the parents of a dying child that their child's deadly disease was there for a reason, or that the person who had just lost their job after 20 or more years of dedicated service just had to find that open door awaiting them, or that the deaths of innocent people at the hands of a kid with an assault rifle was part of a divine plan.

The problem with having a divine plan already set in place for you is that there has to be something or someone who sets that plan in place. If that mighty engineer happens to be an elusive divine being then you might never know for sure what that plan might actually be. Fortunately for you there are plenty of people who are happy to interpret that plan for you–usually to their own benefit. Another problem with a heavenly plan is that there are no alternative possibilities, there is no room for growth and exploration, and there are supposedly terrible consequences for those who do not adhere to it.

The heralding of a sacred plan by an exclusive group of people can make it possible to oppress and marginalize others because often that plan is not meant for everyone. Somehow, only the 'special people' are the benefactors of the master's plan and they use this status as a means to subjugate those who are not. They do this by claiming that people not included in the plan are somehow less than human.

For those of you who read our weekly newsletter, you may have noticed that I provide an opportunity for people to send me spiritual questions with the idea that the answer may become part of a sermon. Well, this is one of those times. Several months ago, someone asked me how it is possible to consider everyone as equally deserving of worth and dignity when there are some people out there who consistently do very bad things. Does a serial killer or a murderous cult leader deserve the same dignity as others? This, of course, comes to the question of evil.

I strongly believe that evil is not something bestowed upon someone. Evil is not a personality quirk that some people possess while others do not. No one is born a killer or an abuser. Though difficult life circumstances and negative influences certainly can be a major factor, it is ultimately bad choices that most often produce harm. As Universalists, we are called upon to separate the choices and the actions of the person. We do not do this for the sake of that person who has caused unspeakable harm and suffering, we do it for ourselves. We do it for the sake of humanity because once we claim that someone, anyone, any class of people, any nation, any culture, any religious community are, somehow, less deserving of dignity–are less than fully human–

we become victims to the same mindset as the perpetrator. It is through this labeling that multitudes of unspeakable horrors have been justified throughout history. There are several contemporary examples in the news I am sure you can think of that demonstrate how that attitude persists even today.

Native North and South Americans were considered less than human when Europeans came to colonize them. People from West Africa were considered less than human when countries like the United States took them from their homelands and made them slaves. Jews as well as trade union workers, gypsies, members of the Jehovah's Witness church, gays, activist priests, and other dissenters were considered less than human and were thrown into concentration camps during World War II. During the Rwanda genocide, the Hutus referred to the Tutsis, many of whom had been their neighbors, as cockroaches who were worthy only of extermination.

All of these perpetrators claimed to know the heavenly plan and who deserved to benefit from it. It is always the holders of the divine plan who are its interpreters and its masters. They are its judges and they determine their own justification for its results.

When I was younger we used to get something called a Triptik before our family went on a vacation. It was a package with a set of maps with clearly marked routes and information about places we could see on the journey. I later found out that the Triptik was nothing but a set of advertisements and the places we were encouraged to see had been paid for and recommended by the sights themselves. The purpose of issuing the plan was not focused on our experiential growth but, rather, on our spending patterns. Regardless, my parents loved their Triptiks because not having a plan was far more inconceivable than being led to local tourist traps. Not having a plan was more frightening than following the given route.

Consider for a moment, however, that there is no heavenly design; there is no celestial contract. It can feel like you're walking in the woods without any signposts or that you're riding in a car with no driver. But, once you've thrown out the Triptik, turned off the online map, shut down the GPS, or gotten off the interstate, you may, at first, feel paralyzed by a lack of direction. I would like to suggest, however, that you find a moment to catch your breath and take another look around. What you may see developing before you is an enormous range of wonderful possibilities and opportunities. Instead of being given directions and dictated principles, you may find new occasions to determine your own growth and meaning. Maybe it's time to step away from the well worn path. Maybe it's time to blaze your own trail or take over the wheel of the car and seek a different road. Maybe it's time to let the map fly off into the wind.

I don't think that everything happens for a reason but I do believe that we can find deep personal meaning and growth in everything that takes place in the winding course of our lives. Instead of thinking that there is a door that opens every time one is shut in your face, I believe there are hundreds of doors all around you that are waiting to be opened. You may need to get up off the floor, find one, and reach for that handle. I do not believe there's a sly guy in the sky drawing up personal plans for us but I do believe that there are a multitude of highways and byways, freeways and roadways, paved trails and dirt pathways that offer us a wide variety of possibilities for us to discover and that each trail has its own set of wonders, joys, challenges, and dangers. That is the mystery and the terror and the beauty and the multifaceted wonder that is a life well lived.

Notes

1. According to the American Automobile Association a Triptik is "an interactive road trip planning tool that can include up to 25 stops" and are still available for purchase.

Sermon 14

Sowing Seeds of Wonder: The Mystery of Emergence

Series: The Emergence of God

Delivered on July 7, 2024

Introduction

This sermon begins as an introduction to the concept of code switching as a way to cross theological and cultural boundaries but then moves on to the dangers of thinking in binaries. One such binary in religion is the idea that the Divine, or God, is separate from Nature. I argue that such thinking can lead to harm and suffering. The initial story is actually an amalgamation of several true stories.

The Sermon

In the fall of 2019, Walter Steadman was dead. He had led an ordinary life. He was a banker and a devoted husband with two children. His wife said that he was quiet, always on time, and a good father to his kids. His family described him as gentle and thoughtful. Naturally, it was a terrible shock when Walter had been found fatally shot at his bank after an attempted robbery had gone very wrong.

Mitchell Hawkins or "Hawk" to his buddies was a freestyle kind of guy. He rode a motorcycle, enjoyed heavy metal music, and was often found on the other side of a beer mug. His friends called him footloose and carefree while his many girlfriends said he was fun and crazy–in a good sort of way. All of that ended one November day when Hawk went missing and was never seen again. The police suspected foul play.

The most curious and perplexing thing about these two disparate stories of lives ending too early is that the authorities also believed they were connected.

Let me tell you another story about the time I moved from Vermont to North Carolina. One day I answered a knock at the front door. A soft spoken gentleman with a heavy Southern drawl introduced himself and welcomed me to the neighborhood. After I thanked him he went on to say that "We in the neighborhood have noticed that you have not cut your lawn in a few days." I explained that I had just started a new job and was very busy. "Well," he went on to say. "I would be happy to take some time to come over and mow it for you." That is what he said. What he meant to say was "You need to cut your lawn right now before we run you out of the neighborhood" but I didn't know that. Instead, when he offered to mow my lawn, I just said "Sure, that would be great." His stone cold face told me that I had made a terrible mistake. There can be some significant differences between Northern and Southern cultures and what I quickly found out was that I needed to learn the art of code switching.

The concept of code switching was first identified and studied in people who could easily switch back and forth between multiple languages. Later, it became a method of changing unique or unfamiliar words and phrases to make them more understandable. In religious discussions, code switching has become a way of helping people of different spiritual traditions understand each other.

For example, when a Catholic friend of mine says to me that "We are all made in God's image," I switch that phrase in my UU mind into one I can more closely understand. I hear: "We are all sparks of one universal flame." When my friend says "I pray to Jesus to absolve me of my sins" I think "I open my heart and mind to compassion and hope". Each is a cultural expression of a deeper truth. I believe that, deep down, every person has the same spiritual needs and aspirations. It's just that years of societal separation have given us different languages and modes of speaking in which to express these yearnings. Code switching is a way to build bridges across unnecessary and unproductive religious divisions.

It is unfortunate that we need such skill at all but, the truth is, that we have been brought up in a world that values separation over collaboration. We form ourselves into disparate groups that each develop their own words and phrases and manners of acting. We are taught that the world is composed of definable opposites such as: day and night, right and wrong, male and female, gay and straight, good and bad, or sacred and secular, just to name a few. Perhaps the most egregious in terms of establishing any hopes for a world of peace and compassion is the perceived opposites of the Divine and Nature.

Now, I am going to stop here and give you an opportunity to practice your own code switching skills. Throughout this sermon, I am going to use the phrase "The Divine" to represent my understanding of the ultimate reality and "Nature" to represent all physical existence. Feel free to change the word "Divine" to God, Goddess, Spirit, Numen, Mystery of Life, or Flying Spaghetti Monster, if you wish. Feel free to change the word "Nature" to Mother Earth, the Universe, the cosmos, physical reality, the Matrix, or whatever word or phrase that works for you.

To continue, I believe the perceived separation of the Divine and Nature has caused countless years of suffering and misery for humans, animals, and the Earth itself. Separation naturally creates a distance between things. Distance between yourself and the Divine means that you must look for it, you must work to relate to it, to understand it, to reach out beyond yourself, and, ultimately, to find your own value. It causes us to see things and other beings as separate from ourselves. It causes us to see some things and people as holy and others as not so sanctified.

It is natural to see things this way at first. We perceive that there is us and then there is everything else–that there is a subject and an object. We experience everything as 'that which is within' versus 'that which is beyond' and objects are either yours or mine. But, this is not the way the world works. Almost everything we know exists on a wide ranging spectrum between polarities. Day and night are not separate but merge into each other. Daylight can contain darkness as darkness can hold points of light. Similarly, what may be right for one person may be wrong for another. The same may be true for the terms good and bad or sacred and secular. We can come to understand that the Divine and Nature are actually two parts of one complete reality. Nature is what we experience while the Divine is the invisible yet no less real aspect of that experience.

To understand this relationship, consider something as seemingly simple as a seed such as a pumpkin seed. Under the right conditions, this seed–no bigger than the end of my finger– will, over time, produce a vine, a large flower, and then a plump round pumpkin much larger than this small seed. How is that even possible? I find myself in a state of awe just contemplating the idea. It seems almost miraculous. The real question and enigma, though, is not HOW this growth happens. We can talk about germination and photosynthesis and cell mitosis and DNA coding and all the rest. The real question is WHY it happens at all. Why?

Have you ever played the 'Why' game with a young person? It's very simple. You start out with a simple statement. It can be about anything and then your young friend asks you why. With each response you provide, you are again asked why. The thing about this game is that no matter how it begins, continuously asking why always leads you to more and more challenging questions. Usually, at some point in the game, the adult becomes so frustrated with trying to provide an answer that they quickly end the game by saying something like "That's just the way it is" which means, of course, "Don't ask me anymore questions".

To bring it back to our little pumpkin seed, we can ask not just WHY it is able to do all the things it does but WHY it does anything at all? Why does this tiny seed develop into a vine, a flower, a fruit, and back into a seed again? Even if it does not become a plant it will become something else such as food for humans or birds or the earth. The one and only thing it will never do is nothing at all. How it evolves is due to its nature and is what makes it thoroughly unique but the why of its existence and transformation is due to its divinity and is what makes it part of everything else. And so it goes for every thing, every plant, every animal, every person, every planet, every galaxy, and every other thing in this enormous universe. Each is distinctive, connected, and sacred. That is the wondrous mystery and miracle of this shared life.

In the story about the investigations of the deaths of Walter, the soft-spoken banker, and Hawk, the carefree biker, an interesting fact led the police to believe that the two cases were intimately connected. It turned out that Walter and Hawk were actually one person who led two very different lives. During the week, Walter tended to the bank and his family while during frequent work trips Walter became the wild and wayward Hawk. The world saw two separate and unique individuals when, in reality, there was only one.

It IS possible to have one divine source that is expressed through a mosaic of diversified forms. It IS possible to understand this one fount of life through a variety of perspectives. It IS possible to say the same truth through a cacophony of interpretations. That is how code switching can be helpful in understanding other viewpoints.

It may be that unity is both the source AND the product of diversity. It may be that the universe is both a canvas AND a painting. It may be that nature is divine while, at the same time, the divine is expressed through nature.

Why is it so hard to see this unity at the base of all this diversity? Why is it so hard to hear the calm whisper of connectedness amidst a howling of opinions? Why must there be so many divergent trails leading from one basic source? Why? Why? Why?

Because that's just the way it is.

Notes

1. The story at the beginning is an amalgamation of true stories combined to make one story.

2. *Sacred Nature* by Karen Armstrong.

3. "Spinoza on God, Affects, and the Nature of Sorrow"

https://cah.ucf.edu/fpr/article/spinoza-on-god-affects-and-the-nature-of-sorrow/

4. "Pantheism: Nature Is God"

https://www.samwoolfe.com/2013/04/pantheism-nature-is-god.html

Sermon 15

The Flooding of Barre

Series: Special Days and Events

Delivered on July 14, 2024

Introduction

This sermon was given within a few days after a serious flood washed out the downtown area of Barre. The flood damaged and destroyed homes and businesses and created lingering health problems for months. It was the third such flood in the timespan of a single year. Before this time, the interval of these events were often in decades but now they were happening at a much greater frequency.

The Sermon

Today I was scheduled to give a sermon on nature and divinity but, as is often the case, the world has changed since I wrote the sermon over a week ago. Nature, it seems, tends to follow its own schedule.

Last Thursday evening I was sitting by my window reading and watching the rain. It started out as a light rain with intermittent clouds but those clouds soon turned into darker clouds and then something much more dangerous. There was a lot of lightning, thunder, and wind and the rain became relentless. Suddenly, a torrent of water came rushing down the hill on a street perpendicular to my own. That street directly led to the house next to ours and a new river that was once a street poured massive amounts of water onto the front porch of that house.

I watched as the water slowly engulfed the land in front of us and then came up to our door. For whatever reason, the water stopped there and over the course of several hours, it receded. When the raging waters had settled down and meandered their way back to the gullies, culverts, and streams from where they came, there was left behind a mountain of stones, mud, tree branches, and despair.

In the last two hundred years, Vermont has had 20 major floods hit the state but not in subsequent years. Last Thursday's event was the third flood in the span of a single year in Vermont.

I did notice this time that we recovered a little bit faster, businesses opened back up a little sooner, and relief efforts were organized a little more quickly and efficiently. It seems we're getting better at floods but that still does not help people who are suffering physically, mentally, and emotionally from the onset of these weather disasters and the pressures they put on people who are just trying to live out their lives.

It is often at times like these that we look to a divine presence for answers and support. When the divine is something 'out there' we look to it for answers. We may ask "Why did this happen?" or "Why wasn't this prevented?" or worse "What did we do wrong to deserve this?" As a Universalist, I do not believe that the divine is separate from everything else. The universe is the divine and the divine is the universe.

What this means is that things do not happen because a separate entity wills them to happen. They do not occur according to some pre-designed plan nor are they the result of a punishment decreed over some sinful act. Nature does as it does because of physical laws. Waters flood our town not because we have done something to offend the big guy in the sky but because the water has nowhere else to go.

If we have caused a transgression it is through our inability to recognize that WE are the cause of the drastic change in climate that has spawned these storms, that WE have taken advantage of nature for a very long time for our own benefit, and that WE have not acted in good faith to repair the damage we have caused. We might not be directly responsible for a natural disaster related to dangerously unsettled weather patterns but we are responsible for conditions that have worsened those patterns and we have done it all in the name of the betterment of humanity. But, humanity can never become better so long as it considers itself separate from the natural world.

As long as we see God as separate from us we will continue to pray for help, we will listen to the voices of those who claim to speak for God, and we will blame people of other religions for our suffering simply because they do not follow the right path. If, however, we can see divinity in every mountain, every river, every being, and every person, then we can no longer blame others. We can no longer seek help from beyond ourselves. We can no longer wait for a solution. We can no longer pretend that it's not happening.

We here in Vermont know firsthand that climate change is real and that it deeply affects our lives in the present. We know that its consequences are significant for people now and we have witnessed how our actions in the past have led to this dilemma. We dug the hole. We fell into it. It is up to us now to pull ourselves out of it and fill it back up. Our belief will not save us but our grief will. Do we sit idly by the celestial phone waiting for the call to come in or do we get up and do what needs to be done?

The divine is not a box in the wall that we plug our appliances into when we need something done. WE are the power we need, WE are the hope we seek, WE are the answer to the questions we ask. I don't mean WE as individuals but the truly collective WE. If nothing else, the divine is more closely experienced when people of good intentions work together for the betterment of all.

What can be more divine than goodness, beauty, and truth expressed through the strength of love? When we work together for the good of all, we bring forth light into the darkness. We are each individual sparks of a greater flame whose brilliance and brightness can only be seen and experienced when those sparks are brought together. Single candles joined together in the dark can create a bright light.

We are the candles. The divine is the light. We have found ourselves in a deep dark cavern and only if we work together will we be able to shine a light and find our way out.

Notes

1. "Why Does Vermont Keep Flooding?"

https://apnews.com/article/vermont-flooding-climate-change-severe-weather-3f1e3c5f55a69cd75d5b5ad0f31792f3

Sermon 16

Emergence: The Blossoming of Beauty

Series: The Emergence of God
Delivered on July 21, 2024

Introduction

The point of this sermon was to demonstrate how emergence develops as two or more things are combined to create something that is more than the sum of the parts. Examples used are the synergy of the original owners of Ben and Jerry's ice cream, water, ants, and jellyfish. The principle of emergence is one of the true great mysteries of our universe in that it, all at once, combines, creates, and unifies.

The Sermon

I once spent my high school summers working as a counselor at a camp for physically challenged children situated in rural Virginia. My first summer spent at the camp meant that I would, naturally, have much to learn. One lesson involved my assignment to help Martin, one of the camp's summer regulars, take a hike on a nearby trail. Martin had no use of his legs and his arms were sometimes difficult to control as well so hiking for him meant being pushed in a wheelchair.

The camp was nestled within the Blue Ridge Mountains and Martin had chosen a route that would take us up a steep trail. I dreaded the idea that I would have to push a wheelchair all the way up the mountain but it turned out that I would not need to do that. You see, when we approached the base of the steep hill, Martin threw himself out of the wheelchair and landed, face first, onto the rocky path. I was mortified. I thought I had failed in my very first camp assignment and that this camper was about to call me every vulgar name known to the English language. But, instead of cursing me, as he was spread out on that pathway, Martin just started laughing.

As Vermonters, I am sure you are all familiar with the story of Jerry Greenfield and Ben Cohen. Jerry was a by-the-book kind of guy. He followed the rules and kept his room neat and tidy. He was cautious and entrepreneurial. He could think of the big picture and he was determined to help people. He wanted to be a doctor but no medical school would take him.

Ben Cohen, on the other hand, was a very different person. He didn't like to follow the rules. He didn't like to do his homework and he was a slob. He was a risk taker and wanted to become a famous potter. His lack of structure and perseverance, though, made it difficult for him to maintain the discipline needed to be a working potter.

The one thing that both of them had in common was that they liked to eat. When they met, they decided to go into business together. Jerry did much of the business work while Ben did a lot of the creative work and together they built one of the most iconic ice cream companies in the world–Ben and Jerry's. Their two different personalities complemented each other. What each person lacked in character was enhanced by the other partner. It is unlikely that either could have accomplished alone what they did together. From these two disparate individuals emerged something greater and more wonderful than was ever present before.

This merging of separate imperfect parts into something that is a greater and more beautiful whole is present throughout nature. We can see it in something as simple as a flower. One flower is often made up of other small petals. Each one is completely different and unique but when combined together they make a highly textured, colorful, and complex flower. It is the amalgamation of all those imperfections that makes the flower so amazing. The same is true with human interactions.

I want to talk to you today about a mysterious force that is active and present throughout our world and the universe. It's called 'emergence' and it affects everything. Emergence happens when two things are combined and from them comes something new. The fascinating thing about emergence is that often something new is created that has properties completely unique to it.

Water is an example of an emergent substance. As you may know, water is composed of two hydrogen atoms that are bonded with one oxygen atom. Hydrogen, on its own, is a very flammable substance. A giant hydrogen-filled air balloon known as The Hindenburg became an enormous fire ball after being hit by lightning. Oxygen is also flammable. In fact, you can't have a fire without oxygen. Modern flame retardants work by robbing a fire of its oxygen source. How is it, then, that when oxygen and hydrogen are chemically combined they produce a substance completely unlike either one of them? Water is used to put out fires. It appears and behaves completely differently from either hydrogen and oxygen.

The mystery of emergence goes beyond material objects, however. Consider ant colonies. The ant brain is more than several million times smaller than the human brain yet ants are capable of acting together in a collective society that works to feed, support, and defend its entire colony–a feat that us humans have yet to learn. They can successfully hunt creatures many times their size and can even construct bridges with their bodies. But, emergent properties in living beings do not even require brains at all. The jellyfish has no such organ and yet can navigate the ocean waters for food and react to changes in the temperature and composition of water. The very poisonous jellyfish known as the Portuguese Man of War is not a single organism. It is actually made up of separate jellyfish polyps that work together as one being.

Emergence happens with human beings as well. Angry mobs, peaceful rallies, labor movements, and flash mobs are examples of groups who can do things not possible by separate individuals. The stock market, inflation, and cultural memes demonstrate patterns of emergent behavior. Perhaps the best example of human designed emergence, however, is the computer.

I am speaking from words written from a computer program. This one compact device can predict the weather, play music, show me more cat videos than I care to see, and can help me stay connected to my congregation. Computers can control home appliances, entire electrical grids, and even all the systems of the international space station. Yet, the amazing thing about all these programs is that they are all based on just two numbers: (Two!) Those numbers are one and zero–that's it. That's how emergence works: you start with at least two unique items and combine them in increasingly complex figurations until new things emerge from them. These new things can then become the foundation for yet even more emergence.

That's the crazy thing about emergence. It doesn't just happen sometimes in a few places and with a few things. It's happening everywhere, with everything and everyone, and all the time. At this very moment, even as I am speaking these words to you, the universe is evolving, the world is changing, and new things and properties are emerging. You will not be the person tomorrow that you are today. When you step out of this church the world will not be the same one you left behind, though it may be hard to notice. This emergence is the basis of the creativity that is happening to everything everywhere all at once. That creativity, that constant renewal, that forever awakening of the universe is the great mystery and, to me, the very definition of the divine.

But there is an even deeper mystery to emergence. Though it is the impetus for the creative introduction of new things, at the same time, it is also the source of unification. With each new development things are combined and merged. Creativity both produces and integrates. It both defines and combines. It generates as well as it incorporates. What is even more intriguing is that we are as much a part of this process as everything else. We are all unique and wonderful parts of this constant universal creativity. And, though we can each bring forth emergent possibilities it is not through our individual efforts that true emergence takes place. When we work together to unite our colony in peace and prosperity, when we meld our hearts together to love all beings, when we join together to protect this planet and all its children, when we see ourselves as part of one dramatic and enigmatic emerging body of creation, THEN we begin to be part of the process of unity and THEN we come that much closer to divinity. Only as one do we come closer to God.

What I didn't know my first summer at the camp for children with disabilities is that Martin, the one who threw himself onto the mountain path and then started laughing, did that same thing every year. It was a ritual for him. He would leap from his wheelchair and then, with the help of all the camp counselors who suddenly appeared on the scene laughing at me, would–with our help–crawl his way to the top of the mountain. He did it every summer because it was the only time that he knew he could get the entire camp behind him, literally. Every summer he would make it to the top and then cry out in tears and joy for having defeated the mountain once again and, every summer, we wept with him. It was something that could only be experienced with the support and encouragement of everyone there, acting together for the betterment of all. Martin showed us that, indeed, it is only as one that we come closer to God.

Notes

1. *Emergence: The Connected Lives of Ants, Brains, Cities, and Software* by Steven Johnson.

Sermon 17

The Cosmic Maybe: Infinite Potentiality

Series: The Emergence of God

Delivered on August 25, 2024

Introduction

In this sermon I discuss an aspect of emergence from a different perspective. In previous sermons emergence is viewed from the bottom up as it expands throughout the universe but there is another part of emergence that is seen by understanding the most likely and most fundamental element of existence which may be not a particle but the pure potentiality of all possible particles and sub-particles.

The Sermon

In previous sermons in this series I have asked you to explore with me the outer limits of understanding. I have encouraged you to expand your awareness to the greatest degree possible. We have seen how all things, all people, all beings, all planets, and everything else is part of one great wholeness that is interconnected, interrelated, interdependent, and marvelously beautiful. We have come to appreciate that we cannot possibly understand everything in this vast and mysterious universe. And, instead of being afraid of this mystery, we have come to realize that we can appreciate and be in awe at those things and ideas we cannot fully grasp.

I have told you that science is the study of nature and the experiential but there comes a point when science cannot answer the bigger questions. Where science ends, spirituality begins. We have done all this by starting where we are and then looking ever outward and upward. We have looked at the big picture as best as we can so that we can appreciate the splendor, the grace, and the utter magnificence of all creation in all its many forms.

I have also encouraged you to try and avoid looking at the world in strictly binary terms. We are brought up in a culture where everything is either this or that. We think that if something is not good then it must be bad or that if something is not right then it must be wrong. But the reality is that most things are not clearly this or that. Sometimes they are both.

Today, however, I want to take you in a different direction. If, as I have claimed, divinity is the sum total of all possible entities in this universe, that it is the mysterious source of all motion and energy that permeates this life and all things known and unknown, that it is the one and only perfection of which all things evolve and seek to become, and that we are all parts of this one great mystical and miraculous wholeness, then through all these images, we may have limited ourselves to only one part of the total picture. We may have only scooped up the whipped cream from on top of the pie without getting to the best part.

We have reached up and out, over and beyond, and to the outer limits of our known world. Conversely, is it also possible that divinity is beneath us, within us, hidden in the tiny cracks, and tucked away in hidden shadows? Could it be that, at the same time, The Divine is the undivided wholeness and the primary ingredient in one great cosmic recipe? Could it be both the sum and the integers in a staggering celestial equation? Could it be, at once, both the castle that is built and the sand that is used to build it?

In 1966, a film entitled "The Fantastic Voyage" was released after years of expensive production. The movie depicted the crew of a nuclear submarine that was shrunk down to about the size of a microbe in order to enter a human body and save the life of the scientist who invented the miniaturization technique. Risking their lives while battling defensive antibodies, pounding heart rates, and gale force breathing, the crew saved the scientist's life just before they regained their normal sizes. With that as inspiration. I, too, would like to take us on a Fantastic Voyage but turn up the controls a bit and shrink ourselves down to the level of a living cell - specifically the Eumycetes. Join me in a fantastic voyage to the world of fascinating fungi.

A fungi is a single-celled organism that has characteristics of both animals and plants. Fungi are important to us in the leavening of bread, the development of antibiotics, the production of natural pesticides, and (this is my favorite fun fungi fact) it is critical in the fermentation of foods such as beer. Our journey might take us within a mushroom where we would see a multitude of tiny hair-like strands that branch out from the cell to reach out to even more strands. These are termed "hyphae". Imagine an octopus. The arms are like the hyphae while the head is like the foundational cell from which they grow. These microbial arms can intertwine to form larger masses such as the entire body, stem, and gills of a mushroom and they can also connect beneath the soil for miles and miles. Furthermore, they can connect to other root structures such as those from trees and plants so that an entire interconnected structure is built underground and used as a way for plants to communicate with each other. This structure is called the mycelium network. Both the mycelium network and the mushroom are living and growing structures derived from the aggregation of smaller living cell structures.

If we could submerge our magical submarine into one of the cells of our fungi we would enter a very strange world. We would find ourselves floating inside a soft membrane with several strange objects floating around us including things like the Golgi apparatus, floating mitochondria, ribosomes, and microtubules. At the center, like the sun in our solar system, we would find the cell nucleus where, like the town library, much of the important information for the cell is stored. More importantly, we would find ourselves inside a separate but interconnected and conscious living being.

My favorite part of submarine movies is when the captain yells "Dive, Dive!" and the ship comes alive with bells and whistles. People run and valves are turned and then the mighty submarine points its nose downward and heads into the deep murky depths of the sea. I would now like us to take our vessel further into the unknown and dive (dive!) deeper until we reach the depth of the thing that makes up all those parts of the cell - the atom.

Strap on your seatbelts, folks, because this is where things get very weird. We have been taught to believe that the atom is like a solar system of ping-pong balls. There is a nucleus made up of at least one proton and a neutron which is surrounded by an orbiting set of electrons. But, if we look out from the windows in our sub, this is not at all what we would see. We may get a glimpse of the nucleus of an atom in the far distance with its conglomeration of protons and neutrons but the electrons moving around that nucleus would probably appear more like a cloud surrounding it. If we are lucky we might see an electron become a noticeable blip for a brief moment like we might see a falling star pass over us at night. That is because the electron is both a physical particle and a non-physical wave of energy. It exists in a world of probability where it is more likely to appear in some places rather than others if it appears at all.

But, what would happen if we were able to delve even further into this mysterious sea of reality? What would happen is that we would probably see exactly nothing–nothing at all. At this unimaginably infinitesimally small realm of existence there would be nothing physical at all to see and yet we would be staring at every possible part of the universe all at once. We would enter what some physicists call the Sea of Potentiality where all particles are invisible waves that reach to every corner of the universe all at once. We might get very brief glimpses of particles that pop into existence for milliseconds like cosmic fireflies on a dark night but nothing would remain unless two or more of those blips happened to connect to each other.

At this mysterious level, everything is possible but only–and this is the most important point–only through interaction and relationship. Nothing develops without interconnection. Nothing exists on its own. And, everything is connected because this primary field of potential is the center, the absolute foundation of everything in the universe. It is a realm that the physicist David Bohm described as "undivided wholeness in flowing movement." It is the One that mystics of all religions seek and describe. It is the greatest and most beautiful mystery.

This infinite potentiality seeks to manifest into stable forms–that is its purpose and it is the purpose of those manifestations to express their full potential. Each part of creation is unique and special yet dependent on continuous interaction for its definition and support. We can think of it as the invisible, yet fully natural, spirit of all things. What we might call The Spirit of Life. Because it exists as the most fundamental and the smallest finite part of all reality it is everywhere all at once. As pure potentiality, it is the source of all creation. It is omnipotent, omnipresent, omniscient, and all-pervading. What could possibly be more god-like than that?

So, the answer to the question of whether the divine could be both the castle and the sand is, I believe, an unqualified yes.

What does this mean for us? That is the subject of the next and final sermon in this series.

Notes

1." Secret Life of Fungi: Ten Fascinating Facts"

https://www.bbc.com/news/science-environment-45486844

2. *Infinite Potential: What Quantum Physics Reveals About How We Should Live* by Lothar Schafer

Sermon 18

So What? Thoughts On The End of a Series

Series: The Emergence of God

Delivered on September 22, 2024

Introduction

This was the final sermon in my series of sermons based on "The Emergence of God." In it I distilled all the ideas in the book and previous sermons to three basic principles. I argue that the actions we take in our lives are motivated by our values and that our values are based on how we view the world and our place in it. This worldview comes from our spirituality.

The Sermon

I am flawed. Like all human beings I am a flawed individual. I have my shortcomings but sometimes you have to learn to let go of the desire to be flawless. For example, I have always had a hard time knowing how to spell or pronounce the word (Ar-Mega-Don) but, instead of being upset by this I say "So I can't spell armageddon. So what? It's not like it's the end of the world." When I was told that someone had stolen all the lamps in my office I said "So what? I'm delighted." When I was told there was a kidnapping at school I said "So what? She'll eventually wake up!" I apologize for the Dad jokes but I wanted to get to the question that children often ask.

Today's sermon is about asking the question "So What?" In the past year I have been giving sermons based on principles I learned and developed while I was in seminary searching for answers about my place in the world. This is the ending of that sequence, the series finale, the one that brings it all together. It is the sermon that seeks to answer the question, (and I invite you to say it with me) *So What?*

I know I am showing my age but I remember when the TV series MASH was going to air its final episode. Now, I could say the same thing about any series closer. Shows like the Sopranos or the Game of Thrones, or the world series, or the super bowl, or maybe some special day you have been waiting a long time to come, have greatly anticipated endings, as do many things in life. For days or months or years we wait for a resolution–an ending to a long succession of events. We anticipate that ending with nervousness or excitement because we believe that something wonderful, something amazing is going to happen.

The series MASH, the show about doctors in a mobile army surgical hospital unit during the Korean war, ran for 11 years. Even today it remains one of the longest running TV shows in television history. It lasted six years longer than the Korean War itself. The series finale was one of the most anticipated shows of its time. It would last for 2 ½ hours and be watched by 125 million people. My friends and I planned a party for the finale and for weeks it was the focus of every discussion so I was shocked when I asked my friend Charles if he was going to watch it with us and he said no. Now this Charles was not that different from the Charles on the TV series. He came from a well-to-do family and was very intelligent but he was also aloof and condescending at times. When I told him about the watch party we were planning he simply and glibly replied, *"So What?"*

'So what' is the question we use when we want to comprehend the significance of something. 'So what' is shorthand for questions like: "So what does this mean for me, for my life, for the people I know, or for the society I live in?" or, even the question,

"Why should I care?" The final episode of MASH was of no value to Charles because he did not watch the show at all so he did not care about its outcome.

Over the past year I have been sharing with you my ideas of spirituality I developed while I was attending seminary. As a UU minister, it is not my intent to convince you that my spiritual understanding should also be yours or that mine is more correct than any other. On the contrary, I simply wanted to explain to you my foundational beliefs so that you know what motivates my words and my actions. If, by chance, anything I share with you may be helpful to you in your own journey, then so much the better.

Although I have introduced quite a few ideas over the past year I want to distill them into three basic spiritual principles. The first is that all beings have value. All people, all plants, all animals, all of earth, and all of the world we know and beyond has meaning and value. We may judge the actions of individuals as foolish or evil or sinful even but the individual will still be an equal part of the fabric of all beings. As we have witnessed in the news lately, trying to make oneself greater by making others lesser is nothing more than a self-serving delusion.

My second principle is that all things are connected. Everything is in relation to everything else in the universe. Everything. All the time. The appearance of separation is an illusion and a consequence of seeing things in binary terms. Rarely is something ever strictly this or that or one thing exclusive of the other. Our universe is constructed through connected polarities, spirals, and fractals. Everything evolves from simplicity to complexity in ways that encourage further growth. That leads me to my third principle.

Principle three is that the universe is in a constant state of creative evolution. Every thing, every day, and every person (including you) is a brand new creation never known or experienced before. Each one is a creative expression of an endlessly changing universe. Creation happens everywhere and all the time so that the universe and every single thing within it are always in the process of becoming something else–something novel and wonderful. What may appear to be constant is simply evolving at a less perceptible rate. Nothing ever remains the same. That, to me, means the universe is one organic and dynamic entity that moves and lives and breathes–not unlike us. That force of constant creativity and expression and vitality is what I sometimes call the Spirit of Life.

But, even after all this talk, all this theological meandering, all this philosophical postulating, each of you will, at some point, probably throw your hands in the air and say *"So What?"* "What does this mean for us?"

Psychologists tell us that the day-to-day actions we take are based primarily on two things they call intrinsic and extrinsic motivation. Extrinsic motivation is caused by forces beyond our selves. When other people tell us what we MUST or SHOULD do or when we follow specific laws, customs, or cultural expectations devised by others, when we are motivated by fear or punishment or the promise of material gain or the need for praise and acceptance, we are motivated by extrinsic influences.

But, when we are driven by intrinsic motivations we do things because we enjoy them or we define ourselves through them or because we believe that we are doing what we believe ourselves to be right. Intrinsic motivation comes from our values and when our actions are aligned with our values we are more likely to experience purpose, meaning, and even joy in our lives. When we do not live through our values, however, we experience what is known as cognitive dissonance. We may feel our lives are disoriented, spurious, without merit, or inconsequential. A life based on positive life-enriching intrinsic values feels more authentic, more fulfilling, and more in harmony with the world.

We can only develop those kinds of positive intrinsic values when we develop our understanding of our place in the world, when we expand our understanding beyond our individual needs, or when we comprehend the nature of our existence. These kinds of values, I believe, are best developed through spirituality. But even now you may be wondering: *So What?*

Here, then, is the answer to the question "So What?" Why do I spend so much time on the value of all beings or on the interconnection of all beings? Why do I speak so much about the endless creative evolution of the universe? Because I believe that these are the spiritual foundations for understanding this beautiful and meaningful universe in which we find ourselves as well as the spiritual foundation for determining how we will live in it. I also believe that the foundation and progress of a just, peaceful, and thriving world comes from those kinds of spiritual values.

If you believe that there is nothing of value in this life then you may come to feel that you have no worth or that others have been given special value. Worse yet, you may come to see others as having less significance than you or your clan and that you may be justified in causing harm to those others. **But**, if you believe that all beings have value for no reason other than because they exist as part of the complete fabric of life, then you may come to appreciate the value of all life.

If you believe that all things are separate and isolated, then you may feel isolated yourself. You may be terribly lonely. Consequently, you might seek only to help yourself. **But**, if you see the world as part of one living breathing web of existence you may come to see yourself as an equally valuable strand of that cosmic network.

If you believe the universe is inert, random, and lifeless, then you may come to feel empty inside. You may find no direction in your life nor even a need to seek one. You may come to see the universe as one large empty clock that just runs on idle inertia and you may come to live your life the same way. You may see the world as devoid of beauty and you might come to treat yourself and others with cold indifference. **But**, if you see the world as a living, evolving, and creative wonder then you might seek to find your own unique expression in this life. You might seek beauty and reverence as you go. You might appreciate the unique and fascinating differences of all things and you might encourage the growth of yourself and all beings.

What we believe matters! It is the foundation of how we come to understand ourselves and our world. It is the basis for all the actions we take in our lives. It is the cornerstone for building social justice, equal rights, and the beloved community. It is the basis upon which we build our lives and the world in which we live.

So, when you ask, *So What?* I say a positive spirituality might just make the difference between a heaven on earth or ar-mega… arma… You know what I mean.

Special Sermons

Special Sermon 1

The Transformation of the Arts

Series: UU Liturgy

Delivered on December 3, 2024

Introduction

This short homily was an introduction to a regular service often done in UU churches known as Arts Sunday. Some churches split up this day and have a separate Music Sunday or Poetry Sunday but We combined it all into one day so that it included music, poetry, movement, visual art, and even a short original play of my own.

The homily used two word ladder puzzles as well as a simple introduction to alchemy to talk about turning hate into love. The word ladder was used as an introduction to the theme of Transformation.

The Sermon

How do you turn lead into gold? For hundreds of years people called alchemists tried to discover the answer to that question. The belief was that all metals are made of different levels of mercury and sulfur and that by manipulating these elements they could be transmuted into any other substance and the most sought after substance was, of course, gold. We assume they were less than successful because people are still searching for gold in the earth rather than freely transforming it in a lab. There are some, however, who still say that you can turn lead into gold through a process that is actually much simpler than firing up chemicals in test tubes.

Here's the secret formula: First, turn lead into mead which is simple indeed. Then let your mead meld into mold before it gets too old. Finally, let that mold sit and grow until that gold can rise and glow. This is an example of a puzzle called a word transformation or word ladder.

> LEAD
>
> MEAD
>
> MELD
>
> MOLD
>
> GOLD

The word 'Transformation', which is our theme for this month, means not just a change but a dramatic change in form or presence. When we think of something that transforms we think of the caterpillar that turns into a beautiful butterfly or of the frog that begins as an egg, becomes a tadpole, and then turns into a frog. When we think of personal transformation we think of a dramatic change in personality or philosophical outlook. An experience that is transformational can significantly change us for better or worse.

We often consider transformation to be a major and occasional earth-shattering sudden change but most transformation takes place over long periods of time and is occurring around us all the time. In fact, everything around us is transforming all the time. The earth, the sky, the galaxy we float in, and the universe itself is constantly in a never-ending process of change. Though things seem to stay the same from day to day this is only an illusion of slow transformations over time but the reality is that nothing ever stays the same. That means there is always hope for us. We can always change, transform, grow, and expand. We can change fear into hope, anger into calm, or suffering into compassion because renewal is the natural progression of this existence we all share. Just like it is possible to change lead into gold, it is also possible to turn hate into love. Yes, it's true. Hate can be transformed into the healing power of love.

HATE
MATE
MOTE
MOVE
LOVE

Special Sermon 2

A Vermont Statehouse Address

Series: Special Event

Delivered on January 31, 2024 at the Vermont State House in Montpelier, Vermont.

Introduction

The Vermont State House of Representatives have maintained a tradition of asking ministers from throughout the state to offer words to start the legislative session. The tradition came from the practice of starting sessions with a prayer but that changed from giving prayers to offering a short presentation. That has come in the form of prayers, songs, poems, or brief sermons. Only three minutes of time is allotted but there is no other restriction made. I chose to talk about the city from which I came and the fact that it had so many granite statues. Barre once had a thriving granite industry that brought to it a great many immigrants from various countries who worked on producing, shaping, and distributing granite statues, memorials, and monuments.

The Sermon

Thank you all for inviting me to speak with you today. It is truly an honor.
I live in Barre - the city of granite. As you know, we have stone monuments everywhere. You can't go far in any direction before you run into yet another granite sculpture. We have

statues of everything: famous authors, airplanes, soccer balls, race cars, armchairs, giant zippers, you name it. All very impressive. All very humbling. Through every flood, every hurricane, and every natural disaster they stand strong and proud. They are monuments of resilience and hope.

Have you ever wondered how those stone carvers do that? How do they turn a gigantic seemingly impenetrable rock into a beautiful work of art? Michelangelo is reported to have said, "Every block of stone has a statue inside it and it is the task of the sculptor to discover it." In other words, a great work is defined by eliminating that which it is not.

I believe there is a lesson in that for us. It may be that we are better defined not by what we are, but by what we are not. Let us consider that we are defined not by our title but how we entitle others. We are defined not by our standing but how we help others to rise. We are defined not by our supporters but by who we support. We are defined not by our religion but by espousing the love and compassion that is the core of every tradition. We are defined not by the money we raise but by the lives we lift out of misery and despair. We are defined not by how we judge through our words but by how we are judged through our actions. We are defined not by how we are knocked down but by how we climb back through the rubble and then reach out to aid others.

All of us are works of art that can be revealed when we chip away at the unnecessary, the hardened, the rough exterior in order to expose the beauty within to become monuments of hope and resilience for others to behold.

Acknowledgement

I wish to thank the Church Council and the members of the First Church in Barre, Universalist for inviting to be their Director of Ministry. It is through that position that I wrote and delivered most of these sermons. I would also like to thank the members of the Acton/Stowe, Massachusetts UU Church who have supported me throughout this process and transition.

Other Books

Non-Fiction

- Spirituality
  - A Different Calling: A Manual for Lay Ministers and Other Non-Professional Facilitators of Any Spiritual Tradition
  - Many Leaves, One Tree: A Collection of Aphorisms Inspired by the Tao Te Ching
  - The Purpose Derived Life: What In The Universe Am I Here For?
  - Three Guidelines for Ethical Living
  - Playing Cards and the Game of Living Well
  - The Emergence of God: The Intersection of Science, Nature, and Spirituality
  - The Langer Deck
  - Emergent Spirituality: Principles and Practices at the Intersection of Science, Nature, and Spirituality
  - Open Hearts and Open Doors: Radical Hospitality in the Church
  - Let Us Wander: A Ministry of Music and Arts
  - Reflections of Reverence: A Collection of Sermons, Book One
- Games
  - 52 New Card Games (For Those Old Cards)
  - 36 New Dice Games
  - 40 Games for Forty Dice
  - Castle Imbroglio: An Escape Adventure Book
- Music

- A Guide to the Art of Musical Performance
- A Theory for All Music
  - Book 1: Fundamentals
  - Book 2: Chords and Part-Writing
  - Book 3: The Tools of Analysis
  - Book 4: Parametric Analysis
- Rounds and Canons for Peace and Justice
- Music for Unitarian-Universalist Choirs
- Songs of Worship
- 50 Songs for Meditation

Fiction

- <u>Science Fiction</u>
  - The Milleran Cluster Series
    - Of Eternal Light
    - The Forever Horizon
    - The Suicide Fire
    - The Song of the Mother
    - The Journey of Awri
- <u>Theater</u>
  - Four Comedies
  - 10 x 10: Ten Ten-Minute Plays Book 1
  - 10 x 10: Ten Ten-Minute Plays Book 2
  - 10 x 10: Ten Ten-Minute Plays Book 3
  - 10 x 10:Ten Ten-Minute Plays Book 4
  - Ageless Wisdom: Multigenerational Plays for Worship
- <u>Poetry</u>
  - Looking At The World: A Collection of Poetry
  - Prayers

Final Note

Thank you for reading this book!

If you enjoyed reading it please let me know and please consider writing a positive online review.

Ken Langer

<u>Contact Information</u>
personal website: http://kennethplanger.com
book site: http://brassbellbooks.com
Email: revklanger@gmail.com

www.ingramcontent.com/pod-product-compliance
Lightning Source LLC
LaVergne TN
LVHW011205080426
835508LV00007B/606